THE
LASCAUX REVIEW
VOLUME 9

ANNO DOMINI 2022

THE
LASCAUX REVIEW
VOLUME 9

ANNO DOMINI 2022

edited by
Stephen Parrish
Wendy Russ

The Lascaux Review

Editor
Stephen Parrish

Managing Editor
Wendy Russ

Senior Editor
Shannon Morley

Editors
Isabella David McCaffrey
Erica Orloff
Lisa Pellegrini
Sarah Specht

ISBN: 978-1-7344966-4-2

Cover design by Wendy Russ. Cover art by Arthur Streeton: "Sunflowers," oil on canvas, 1926.

Lascaux Books
www.lascauxbooks.com

Contents

continued next page

Poetry (continued)

Short Fiction

Creative Nonfiction

Crystal Pigs
by Allison Brice

We swore never to use our customer service voices in bed. It kept us vulnerable and that made the sex good (awkward, and often prone to crying, but good). With her I could be myself, could exist in all my awkwardness and strangeness and reject the initial impression of my boots and jacket and shaved head. And as it turns out she was even weirder. Turns out that my straight-passing librarian girlfriend watched a lot of deeply weird anime and collected Swarovski crystal animals like a grandma. They weren't particularly valuable, only a couple hundred bucks each, but that's a lot for a county employee. So she searched all over the internet for deals, with an eye as discerning as a jeweler. When she found the prize—a tiny crystal pig with a spiraling glass tail, a hedgehog with pokey spikes—it was a celebration, a glass of good wine ($16.99) popped in her room, as she lovingly added the new family member to the overladen shelf. If her antidepressants weren't acting up we'd have sex. And with my head against the pillow and her hair tickling the insides of my thighs, I'd look up and see a hundred sightless black glass eyes watching me.

We fell in love softly (easily, quietly, over games at the arcade bar and cheap lagers), and we fell apart softly (silently, awkwardly, dinners with nothing to say). She stopped talking to me, started watching me like she was waiting for something, and how was I supposed to know what that was when she wouldn't tell me? And when the sex stopped working I didn't want to tell her that whatever new thing she was trying with her tongue was ineffective and did she even know where the clitoris was? But that was so mean, so instead I said *Yeah babe, that's good* and her head popped up because she'd been to my restaurant and she knew what I sounded like when I was reciting drink orders back to a table and the next morning over coffee she said it wasn't working.

And it was fine, a very calm and mature breakup. It was fine, and it was miserable hell. A pierced tattooed dyke with Doc Martens yet I took my breakup quietly, like a pitiful February rain with no lightning. Without her, the existence that I'd carved for myself showed its emptiness, showed all the corners where she used to be, grinning at me with her dimples and holding my hand while she fell asleep, like an otter.

She was a statue, tall and strong, complete unto herself. I was a handful of crumbled gold dust that had once been someone.

The rains came, springtime and petrichor and washing away. But fine wasn't really fine. And it occurred to me that

2

what she wanted was a commitment, a pledge, a partner rather than a girlfriend. And how better to prove it than by buying her the hummingbird, the one crystal animal she'd always searched for.

Except it was $829 fucking dollars.

That was a month's rent and utilities. No wonder she'd hunted for a deal, who could afford that? But what else could I get her, what else would get her to even look my direction?

The thing about working in the restaurant industry is that you meet people. And then they meet people, and you all talk over shift drinks at the end of the night, and suddenly you've got a guy who knows a guy who can get you what you need at a discount. And three traded shifts and most of my savings later I had the hummingbird in hand, walking up to the coffee shop where she agreed to meet me.

She sat outside in pink Keds sipping a latte. Her unshaved legs said *I don't care* but her perfectly threaded eyebrows said *Someone insulted me in middle school and I wear it like a battle scar.* She looked up when I came crunching up the pathway and while I was still a good four steps away I launched into my prepared take-me-back-I-love-you speech, topped off with a presentation of the hummingbird glinting in the light.

Instead I heard, "This was always the problem with you."

No, I protested, but the hummingbird—

Who cares about the hummingbird, she said, in the harsh voice she normally reserved for her mother. You didn't actually care who I was or what I liked, you just wanted someone to be with you and it didn't matter who that girl was. Six months and I don't think you ever met my friends, ever visited me at work, it was all *I love the way you make me feel* and *I love your body beside me* and I'm more than just a body, okay? I'm more than just someone to be there next to you and make you feel whole.

The other patrons of the coffee shop watched in fascination as my face fried up. That's not true, I wanted to protest, I also love the way you cheer me up after a long day, and the way you helped me do my taxes, and your smile when I talk about the stupid people at work...

Oh.

She watched this realization wash over my face, and I could see her struggle with herself, the desire to soothe it away, absolve me of my guilt with her people-pleasing heart. She had to bite her lip to hold the words in.

"So I guess it's a no, then?" I asked.

Still she said nothing. Suddenly feeling very awkward—like every one of my fingers was a fat, flaccid sausage—I put the hummingbird down on the metal table. The blue body of the bird caught the light and splashed a rainbow across her knee.

She reached out and let the beak press into her fingertip.

Career Change

by Lisa K. Buchanan

The mortician arrived last night, well before the viewing, to paint our little girl pretty. He was not the expected somber-suited officiant, but a bearded hippie with sunglasses and an art background. His former career, a renowned painter of psychedelic album covers, peaked before our girl was born, but he has since created an extensive portrait gallery of women with lush and wavy tresses, clingy drapery over limber angularity, and just enough exposed flesh (well, perhaps more than enough) to titillate. His subjects' shadowy faces—arsenic-pale, holy and transcendent—approach the next world with beguiling solemnity.

Our girl has chlorinated laps for breakfast, a climbing wall for lunch, and a treadmill for dinner, gripping handlebars her collar bones now resemble. Her legs look storky; her complexion, ghoulish. Meanwhile, her womanly-hipped friends gab over burritos after tacking up posters in dorm rooms.

As a model, she tells us, she has found her niche.

I suppose we ought to take the long view and find some consolation in today's artiste, because long after the starving and shivering are over, we'll have our girl's image framed and hanging in our living room: her bony white shoulders and bony white knees; her skeletal fingers holding a white bouquet; her dark, downward gaze on all who enter; a tribute to the grim, famished figure a painter saw as beauty.

"Career Change" originally appeared in *Narrative*.

Museum of Grand Gestures
by Danielle Claro

Scavenged lectern, 2012
Wood, dirt, brass

This piece, rescued from the side alley of a brownstone on 117th street in New York City, was carried by hand on a commuter train 30 miles north to the village of Sleepy Knoll. It was then lugged a quarter mile on foot and delivered to the front porch of a woman who had once off-handedly expressed the desire for a standing desk. When the recipient arrived home from work the night of her 35th birthday, it is reported, she was frightened by the silhouette of the lectern, having mistaken it for an upright raccoon. Two weeks after the wobbly item was delivered, it was again among bags of trash. Some say it stands to this day in the garage of Sleepy Knoll's Municipal Department, occasionally displaying a box of baked goods.

Inscribed compact disc, 1999

Polycarbonate plastic, indelible marker

Liz Phair was a U.S. singer of some repute in 1991, when the recipient of this Grand Gesture attended a concert, in San Francisco, California. At the time of receipt, some years later, the victim was pregnant with her second child, who herself would one day take the stage as a singer. The gift represents an apology by a husband for what appears to have been some sort of financial transgression. Papers do not reveal details, but experts believe the misstep to have been significant. The CD displays a pointed plea, in the celebrity's hand. Scholars consider this work exceptional in the category, due to its alarming specificity and the collaboration of one who could reasonably be considered a "rock star." This Grand Gesture was accepted with some degree of humiliation but was clearly valued, as it was preserved by the recipient in the sturdy Ziploc material common to the era.

Homemade *"Don't"* flag, 2005

Acrylic spray paint on pima cotton

Though liberals in the mid-90s were adamantly pro-choice, there existed within this population a discernible discomfort regarding elective abortion for women in committed relationships. Many progressive middle-class marrieds who already had children, even those facing a high risk of divorce and/or severe financial insecurity (see previous work), were expected to soldier on with unplanned pregnancies, falling back on the refrain, "What's one more?" This cloth flag highlights an urging from an unemployed husband to his wife of seven years, when she became unexpectedly pregnant soon after the birth of their second child. Financial struggles (recorded) made the wife's choice understandable if not without pain. She headed to the doctor to terminate the pregnancy medically. It is unconfirmed but said that the husband chased the wife to the subway in the Brooklyn borough of New York City, descended to the far-facing platform and opened this bedsheet-flag the width of his outstretched, upraised arms. The flag read, simply, "DON'T." It is widely believed that the couple divorced three years later.

Carved sidewalk square, 1983
Concrete, water, forefinger
Lincoln Center, a cluster of midcentury buildings providing a home for the arts on Manhattan's Upper West Side, was designed by iconic architect Eero Saarinen in the mid 1950s. It remains a hub of dance, classical music, theater, and film today, although recent events indicate a high probability of mixed-use zoning in the very near future. This concrete sidewalk square, poured in the summer of 1983, sat between Avery Fisher Hall (now David Geffen Hall, and originally Philharmonic Hall) and Columbus Avenue, which serves as eastern perimeter for the complex. Under cover of night, it was crudely carved with two sets of initials joined with a plus sign, in the traditional manner. The next day, it was revealed to the recipient, a dancer of adult age who, according to letters and diaries, walked on the opposite side of Columbus Avenue ever after.

Rough-hewn urn with ashes, 2017

Clay, glaze, human remains

Crafted in Taos by a ceramic artist who specializes in primitive renderings of desert animals, this coiled pot (plus contents) is arguably the most important work in the collection. It's a fine study in humble presentation and long-lead commitment. The recipient—a woman in her late 40s, according to most estimates—lived alone. Scholars believe, based on strong evidence, that she had received two padded envelopes from a bereft former lover in the year prior. This item arrived in a small Amazon box two days before Christmas. Whether planned or coincidental, proximity to the holiday (plus the familiarity of the box's logo) normalized the package, heightening its ultimate impact. "Unboxing" (to use the parlance of the time) was not witnessed. However, it is safe to assume that upon breaking the seal, the recipient would have seen a layer of silver tissue paper—another signifier of ordinary holiday goods. She would most likely have lifted the small covered pot out of the packaging. At this point, we must lean into conjecture. Either the recipient removed the coarsely fitted lid, peered inside, and saw a fair quantity of gray ash against the pale glazed interior of the vessel, or she found the note nested in the hollow of tissue paper left by the pot. The note was written in shaky felt-tip pen, most likely by a left-handed female:

"In my brother's letter, he said this should go to you."

Employing every classic device in the Grand Gesture toolkit—surprise, understatement, third-party participation, slow reveal—this work is a stellar model for students of the form. A major posthumous achievement.

Paper Saints
by Tommy Dean

I might as well admit that I'm sinking. You know the joke about lifeguards drowning? Rip currents don't care who they plunge to the bottom. Lake Michigan, a beast, roaring, devouring. Only in death, sanctifying. All sins washed away in the black print of your name in the paper.

The water thrashes around me; a movie I can't pause. I'm separating from my body, each neuron a dry fire against the inevitable. Muscles ache and tingle as arm after arm goes out and into the delicate skein of the water.

I had laughed through the training videos. The mothers always so sad. Each one of them saying "He was a beautiful soul. A kid any mother would be happy to have. He was just starting to figure things out." Then, on cue, they point to a row of trophies and certificates decorating the deceased's room. They always zoom in on some goofy photo. A trip to

Disneyland, a bike ride for diabetes, picking up trash on the highway.

Me? I'm a fuck-up extraordinaire. Swimming by myself, at night, half-high, the stars smeary like the headlights through a rain-soaked windshield. I'll live forever or I won't, the odds pointing toward something violent, painful, anything but boring. But alone?

Tired? Like a marathon runner stumbling through those last fifty feet, gravel scarring their knees as they crawl through the finish line. The water a swirl of limbs grasping, slicing through, tunneling me under each time my arm fails to complete the next stroke.

A message? Tell my mother not to use my senior picture, to find the one with my hair dyed blonde, my tongue out, hands air-jamming on an invisible guitar. Don't let her find the ones where I'm drunk. Skin bruised, waxy like an apple left out in the sun, a riot trying to escape. Burn those. Let those be the ashes you scatter anywhere except over water. No more water; there's nothing holy there. Back to the photos. Oh, that one from kindergarten, with the cowlick and the square teeth, the dimples. You could add a freckle or two. Make it look wholesome. She'd like that.

Letter to My Coroner
by Christina Litchfield

We meet on a Monday—I would never die on a weekend. You hate Mondays because the weekend means car accidents and those are often tricky and unpleasant. Tuesdays are much better, as Mondays are for suicide (who could blame them?) and those are much more straightforward. You push your briefcase or your purse into the locker and suit up for the day's festivities. I've been waiting for some time but I'm not going anywhere. Pfft.

You were a child when you were interested in taking things apart, even if you couldn't actually put them back together. You cut the worm in half and stared in shock, realizing that there was no way to mend the damage, no way to reverse the action you so recklessly took. You proclaimed to your parents in your senior year—I'm going to be a medical examiner. You mean a coroner? Maybe it was to prove that you could observe the mutilated worm without being the one who inflicted the pain. Maybe you became a coroner to avoid becoming a serial killer. I won't judge.

You pull the drawer open and the tag swings. I have perfect toes that dug into the soft sand of the Pacific, the Atlantic and maybe back again. I often thought about what you'd think of me. My awareness of lying here stretched out for your inspection stilled my hands many times they reached for something fattening, high-calorie, headed straight for my thighs. I never wanted to disappoint. Your mother sometimes calls you a diagnostician when people ask what kind of doctor you are. Ouch. The crescent-shaped scar you'll find on the back of my left heel got there when I was eight and breaking up a fight in the parking lot of my apartment building. The girl was bigger than me and her victim but I could reach her hair and drag her to the ground. I learned that fury at injustice can hide pain. You know that we build tolerance to most anesthetics.

My hands are soft and cold, dainty fingers that wanted to but didn't play the piano. When you were in elementary school you took lessons; they weren't as interesting as the worms. There's a long scar on my right calf, like the serrated edge of a knife or the scalpel you hold; I have no clue how it got there but I always liked the mystery. Your hands are steady. When I was done having babies I went to Miami for a tummy tuck and—funny story—almost died. That long purple slash of a scar low on my belly is hard to miss. Kids and their aftermath are dangerous. You have a child someday but find that birth can't outweigh death. It follows you to the break room and to your car and to your sister's wedding where you say you're a diagnostician when people ask what kind of doctor you are.

There is nothing else remarkable except for three tattoos that faded with sun and age. The Chinese characters on my right forearm—you take a picture with your phone so you can ask a friend to translate—mean "the fragrance of plum blossoms sharpens in the bitter cold." I chose that one to ground me, so I could read it over and over late at night when I taught English to Chinese people and wanted nothing more than to run away. I didn't run away. You like the black roses on my left shoulder, ones chosen just because they were beautiful. Sometimes beauty is enough. The swirling phoenix on my right shoulder blade appeared because it had been me or could have been me or I wanted it to be me. I want it to be me. You trace your fingers along the red ridge of a flickering wing. You get a tattoo just like it next year. You want it to be you.

Some Things You'll Do When You Would Rather Be Happy

by Laurie Marshall

You'll check the mailbox one last time in case there's an unexpected windfall waiting to pay the mortgage, or an official announcement that the whole thing was a sick joke or that there's a new technology that can bring someone back to life just like in the movies and your life is not, in fact, forever changed. Today the mailbox is empty.

But before the mailbox, you'll drive down the dirt road and away from the house one last time looking to see if there are blackberries on the canes, listening to the crunch of rock under tires through the open windows and inhaling the dust deep into your lungs where you invite it to nestle in, to become thickened and scarred over, visible on x-rays as tiny white dots in otherwise translucent flesh. To become a physical part of you.

But before the drive, you'll lock the red wooden door one last time and pocket the key that you have no intention of handing over to the man at the bank or the eventual new owners but will, instead, wear on a chain around your neck because it is a literal key to your truth and your personhood and the floor plan of your life up to this point. They'll change the locks anyway.

But before you lock the door, you'll say goodbye one last time to the dogwood outside the window over the kitchen sink where you learned to peel potatoes, and the fireplace built of stones warmed by the sun on this land and placed by the hands of your grandfather, and the bathtub where your mother bathed each night before bed and where she landed after the fall that preceded the news that she had a mass in her right parietal lobe. This would explain the question about her sobriety when she was pulled over six months earlier.

But before you say goodbye to the dogwood and the fireplace and the bathtub, you'll say goodbye to your mother one last time as she lies unconscious and numbed by morphine, her skull leasing space to an assassin that doesn't care about trees or stones or keys or the agony that its residency is causing and will continue to cause once it, and its host, have stopped breathing and are burned to ashes and blown downriver from the edge of the limestone bluff salted with fossils of creatures that are alive only in our memories and imaginations.

The Wild Plums are Blooming

by Mark Schimmoeller

The wild plums are blooming. They have bloomed every April since the man moved into the woods. The wild plums are blooming, a whole universe of them, and, God, every beginning of April, they block out the horrors of the world. The bees are there too, and he can't hear the horrors of the world when the bees swarm the wild plums at the beginning of April.

The wild plums are blooming the year after epic fires across the globe. The man takes his chair outside to sit under a universe of wild plum blossoms and the humming of the bees until nothing remains but the blossoms and the bees.

The wild plums bloom the next year too, and the man is sitting in his chair under the blossoms and the humming of the bees, and now a sleek black pistol rests on his lap. The stain of a cardinal inside the white blossoms shocks the man, and the humming of the bees under the blossoming trees is a balm to his brain.

The wild plums are blooming, but it's March. The world is off, yet the man is there under the blossoms, waiting for the bees, desperate for the humming of the bees. Come insects, come, everything has bloomed too early. The world is off, it fails us.

The man puts his hand on the sleek black pistol, and a zebra swallowtail lands on the barrel, so close to the man's hand. It raises its black and white wings and lowers them, raises them, and lowers them, so slowly, like it's the first time it has tried its wings, like it has just emerged from its chrysalis, and maybe anything then can be a stamen with nectar, even the barrel of a sleek black pistol, as the man sits under the blooming plums, until all that remains is the blooming of the plums.

Directions Back to Childhood

by Judith Waller Carroll

Turn left at the first sign of progress
and follow the old highway
along the Stillwater River.
When you hear the whistle of the train,
take a right and cross the covered bridge
that leads to the rodeo grounds
where the silver-maned bronc
caused so much havoc the summer you were ten
and the ghost of your grandfather's jeep
rests behind the bleached-out grandstand
choked with blackberries.
As you round the corner into town,
there's a white picket fence
laced with lilacs. Walk through the gate.
You'll see a blue and white Western Flyer

lying on its side in the middle of the sidewalk.
It will take you the rest of the way.

"Directions Back to Childhood" originally appeared in *Zingara Poetry Review*.

First Nail

by Brendan Constantine

I take your portrait down to clean
and notice the scar of another
hanging, painted over. Whoever
lived here before also put a picture
on this wall, looking into the room.
It's an old building. I remember
the landlord saying that over and
over as if it explained something,
the plumbing, the tile, the deaths
of people we love. And if it really
was "near a hundred years" then
there wasn't just one picture before
yours, there were many. I've never
wanted a time machine so I could
stop assassinations or feed french fries
to dinosaurs, but I want one now,

want to set it before your lost smile
and watch the pictures change. No
telling into what: another person
or ten raising glasses, a faithful
dog, maybe Christ. Of course, there
must've been things, too: a calendar,
a coat peg, a little shelf for a candle.
But, I bet it's mostly faces and
dear ones. That's what you put on
a wall like this, that's who should
greet you when you come home
from a wrong day. I would stop
the machine when the building
began to look new, just before
the first nail. Then I would run it
forward again and make a poem
of time, so that every picture—all
the saints or sailboats, all the wild-
eyed babies—digressed to you.

In Her Last Days

by Peter Dudley

Another email
shorter than the last
an alphabet strewn
in bits and batches
letters disordered
words mutated

the white space

like gasps

the chemo has burned out
and hospice watches
with tender eyes
and when all the words
drip down the screen

and an evening breeze
lifts mourning dove song
through my open window,
I hear her whispering
from miles away,
"I am so tired."

Thirteen

by Rebecca Foust

I was thirteen, and there was a boy's mouth
where my legs met. My heart beat

like a bird caught in a bag, let's say
for her plumage. I could smell his want,

thirteen and there was a boy, and I became
something salt and sweet

where my legs met. My heart like a bird
swelled and split

the clear air with its song. I was the must,
the first press wine,

thirteen, and only this boy and the needles
under the pines,

that cedary bed, fragrant and ancient as dust
and where my legs met—thirst—

a boy, my heart like a bright, caught bird.

"Thirteen" originally appeared in *Arts & Letters*.

Saving Sgt. Billings

by Kari Gunter-Seymour

We did what we could,
hid the bottles, drove what
was left of him deep
into the yawning hollow,
built a campfire, drank water
from a long-handled gourd
a galvanized bucket.

We set up tents for triage,
counted his breaths, worried
over irregular heartbeats,
sweats, persistent vomiting,
his jacked up adrenal system.

We waited. Listened for a canvas
zipper in the night, each long slow
pull a call to duty, our legs folding
over duct taped camp stools,

tucked tight around the fire,
his gut-fucked stories, stenched
in blood and munitions,
overpowering the woodsmoke's
curling carbons.

Crows haunched on branches
behind our backs, sentinels,
silent as we wept.
We doused him in creek water,
a sharp sheen of moon over our bones,
recited communions, sang songs
our mothers taught us in the womb,
every neighbor dog and coyote
within earshot barking hill to valley.

Some people think they
don't deserve to be loved,
every story scratched
into the dirt an ache.
That week, down in the lower forty
we all got born again.
It was hard to say who saved who.

"Saving Sgt. Billings" originally appeared in *Cutleaf.*

Five Pieces to Assemble After the Quarantine

by Molly Lanzarotta

1.

The lover who decides to stay understands—like you,
standing too close on the train—it's all about
the distance we keep, or give away.

2.

At the roadside shrine the cash machine's eyes
spy our indulgences, our withdrawals and confessions.
Masking-up becomes escape into disguise.

3.

We say to the faith healer—there are some situations
a cure cannot mend. We say to the traveler—
take care, transience can become transformation.

4.
From a plane, you glimpse fireworks from the top;
like dandelions, they blow and spread. Like near-death,
illuminated, you wonder where it stops.

5.
How long do you allow, to catalogue loss?
How long will you wait, to do what comes next?
You climb up from the rut, spit out the dirt, and
plant what it costs.

Gratitude

by Scudder Parker

The peonies and gladiolas are more
seductive every fall. I choose slips

of peony root with three buds full
of color that may prosper years from now.

I dig shaggy gladiola corms,
plumped on slender stalks, next year's

replacements for the tough exhausted husks
left from the thrust of color-trumpets to the sky:

purple (steeped in black), regal crimson,
slim white Abyssinian, lavender

that cried out to sunset orange;
bulblets cling, intent on futures of their own:

Beauty's nonchalant kindness
accepts the slow learning of my eyes.

A few days of October sun—they seem
like gratitude, always a surprise.

I plant the slips; come in and sort the corms;
possessed by past and future blooms.

I remember how I dreaded
grownups who creaked like closing doors.

Even now I fear joy might never
be allowed back through my window,

but gratitude's a different eye that opens—
unnerving in its great permissions.

In sun, on this cold porch, I'm grateful.
Some shy part of me is always

sitting here, no wisdom, no plan; full
of psalms, no notion who I'm singing to.

"Gratitude" originally appeared in *Crosswinds Poetry Journal.*

The Poem of the World
by Scudder Parker

The poem of the world
    reveals itself
like a doe's hoof tapping ice
till she can drink.

Startles like the rust of purple on this fall's
forsythia leaves, though it may have used that small voice
every year, unheard.

Blinks like red and blue potatoes,
dug this morning, drying in the sun, testing
their startled untrained eyes.

It's the unexpected tickle, the fit of shared
laughter in our urgency of touching that becomes
another way of making love. It's an ocean

35

beach of pebbles that suddenly
starts singing, each stone its own tink;
together, a glorious indifferent song.

And it's the voice of each bird I have only heard
as morning chorus landing with its own song
and bright perfect body in my brain.

It is even—now I begin to see them—the subtraction
of birds, taking summer with them, too busy
to announce their leaving.

The poem of the world wants me to wake
in my own body; it is astonished I might let
these supple bones grow brittle.

It is the sudden thing I trust.

"Poem of the World" originally appeared in *Crosswinds Poetry Journal.*

Three Prose Poems

by Kathleen Rooney

Down

This day could use the excitement of receiving a surprise package. Even better if that package reads THIS SIDE UP.

Don't tell me to take this frown and turn it upside down; it's my frown and I can do what I want.

I went to high school in Downers Grove, founded in 1832 by Pierce Downer. I have zero knowledge of his temperament, but I hope that his surname becoming an eponym cheered him.

Would you find it odd if I asked you to sit down and talk about the existence of God? It would serve me well to know

the meaning of hell. I will tell you, "Wow, that's so deep."
And you will say, "Let me break it down."

Astrologers down the ages have lain down on the ground to
study a patch of sky from below, their lore passed down by
word of mouth.

If you need to calm down, try running up and down the
stairs. Pacing up and down the room. Walking down to the
lake.

You look ravishing, darling, with your hair down like that.

D.W. Griffith was racist and a mess as a director, but I
watched all two hours and 27 minutes of *Way Down East* just
to gaze at Lillian Gish and Richard Barthlemess.

A neutral adverb, "down" gets placed in a lot of masculine
contexts: gridiron football and its countless dull downs. He
downed that whole six-pack like an enemy aircraft. Okay,
you're a man, we get it, settle down.

A massive dude parks his blue pickup truck on the corner,
radio blaring a country station. I want to yell out the window,
"Hey buddy, turn it down!" But I'm afraid he'd gun me
down.

Riding high from her sleeper hit *Mean Girls*, Lindsay Lohan
was the host of *Saturday Night Live* the night Rachel Dratch

premiered the character Debbie Downer. From the heights of fame the only place to go is down.

Hey babe, while you're up, can you pull down the shade? While you're at it, can you burn down the patriarchy?

The minor third interval of the Sad Trombone consists of four descending notes. A plunger mute helps, because a soupçon of comedy is the quintessence of failure.

Thinking about down comforters really brings the ducks down.

The emotional impact of the statement "the system is down" hinges entirely upon the system in question.

Death can be such a lofty concept that it helps to bring it down to earth, like: how many miles of toilet paper will I have used in my lifetime?

It's getting down to the wire for the human race. But there's always time to get down on the dance floor.

I'll drink to that—down the hatch.

*

Can

The Little Engine that Could began as a sermon. I haven't read it in a while. Does it hold up? Is it any good? Can we agree that optimism and hard work have their limits?

Congress can declare war. But Congress shouldn't.

I cannot even with America right now.

Growing up in rural Nebraska, one of seven kids in a family that couldn't afford a piano, my dad played the accordion. His favorite piece was Jacques Offenbach's "Can-Can." I can picture him—rambunctious, bumptious—cantering around, booming the tune until his own dad cantankerously told him to can it.

That canny physical and metaphysical resonance whenever I say, "Can you open this can?"

Keep that up and you're going to get canned. But maybe getting canned is not the worst that can happen.

"I-think-I-can-I-think-I-can"—I'm a capitalist subject, so of course I'm meant to think that.

Extravagant postures, lascivious gestures—as dances go, the can-can is hysterical. The song's real name is "Galop infernal," devised for the final act of *Orpheus in the Underworld*,

40

meant to evoke drunken gods partying in hell. It captures that well. Risqué high kicks! Splits! Cartwheels!

A can of peaches, a can of ability. Can you really eat that whole can of beans?

To conclude her can-can, La Goulue bent over and tossed her skirts over her back to reveal the heart embroidered upon the seat of her underwear. This move came to be known as "the derrière."

Almost nothing actually comes in a tin can. You probably mean aluminum.

Everything money can buy and everything money can't. You can't drink oil. You can't eat profits.

He locked himself in the can and refused to come out. I hope that the cops never throw you in the can.

My high school speech team mentor Melissa got me a coffee mug that said *If you can believe it, you can achieve it.* She bought it from a shop in the mall called Successories. Commodity fetishism at its suburban peak, but in my head, I started telling myself stories about winning anyway. Then guess what? I did.

Physically or mentally able, indicative of possibility. Maybe every elected official needs a kick in the can.

41

You can go now if you like.

Rapturous, sublime, and over in 2 minutes and 11 seconds' time, here's hoping they play "Can-Can" at the end of the world. Can you imagine?

*

Rain

Rain again. Does that rhyme when you say it?

Gray clouds gauze the wounded sky. Peculiar beauties in a heaven full of specimens!

Luke Howard taxonomized in his "Essay of the Modifications of Clouds": cirro-form from Latin for *curl of hair*, cumulo for *pile*, strato for *layer*, and nimbo for *rain*. Goethe, beset with an almost painful admiration, popularized these classifications in a poem: "My winged song thanks / the man who distinguished cloud from cloud."

I bless the rains down in Africa—I love that stupid song.

Acid rain corrodes my dreams like statues. Rain of terror in an era of global weirding.

Clouds cover 2/3 of the planet at any moment, but as the Earth warms these clouds become scarcer. Fewer surfaces reflecting the sun back to space means the Earth gets even warmer, which leads to even fewer clouds. Tufts brushed aside like cotton from a bottle.

Thunder gallops across the sky, but the earth remains dry. My kingdom for some rain!

A reign usually lasts until the monarch dies. Will humans abdicate? Will we be deposed? The monarch butterflies are dying.

A headline in *Scientific American* last month: "Eight States are Seeding Clouds to Overcome Megadrought." Though little evidence shows that the process increases rain.

Maybe if we wrest the reins of government from corporations? Maybe if we give free rein to our imaginations? *We must keep a tight rein on spending,* we're told.

Each plasma cell in the sun is about the size of Texas. Useless to know, perhaps, but morbidly fun.

In *The Merchant of Venice*, Portia says, "The quality of mercy is not strained; / It droppeth as the gentle rain from heaven / Upon the place beneath. It is twice blessed; / It blesseth him that gives and him that takes." We've taken too much. It's too late to correct our mistakes.

The golden sun, a timepiece overhead, counting us down.

A Kurt Schwitters poem in its entirety: "When I am talking about the weather / I know what I am talking about." That was what, a hundred years ago?

A glissando of rain gives way to the pecking beaks of pizzi-cato violins. The soundtrack indicates the nearing of the end.

I don't even know anymore.

Satin Nightgown or Flannel Pajamas
by Claire Scott

Suspended between lover and caregiver and not doing either especially well. I prefer neat piles, no quarters in the

heap of nickels, no spoons in the section for forks, no screws in the mason jar of nails or thumbtacks in the box of pushpins.

But some things don't sort simply. You ten years older, your body bent, shuffling like a polar penguin, misremembering names and passwords, taking eight prescriptions a day.

Angry I have to change light bulbs, fill birdfeeders, fertilize tomatoes. Angry you forget your hearing aids, your heart beats too fast and doctors appointments fill our days.

But I see the gladdest smile when I come home, like summer heat shimmering off asphalt. We watch *Before Sunrise*, my

head on your shoulder, falling asleep on the ancient sofa
where we made love many times ago.

The cold coin of December waits, knowing its turn will come.
We read Mary Oliver, listening for the phone's chime, signal-
ing time for Aricept and Lisinopril.

Time for satin pajamas or a flannel nightgown and dreams of
nickels waltzing with nails, forks sashaying with pushpins.

Caney Fork

by Annette Sisson

Autumn crisps the tapering light,
oak pulls on its auburn duster.
We drive beside the river to the steep
    orchard where apple trees climb
the furrowed ridge. In fall we recall
    how the tang of applesauce, as native
and ardent as old marriage, staves off
    winter's crisis of ice. En route
we wonder: Will the bent woman
    still be there? Or will she have joined
the earth somewhere between hollow and hill?

You find the crack in the dell, nose
    our car down the dirt drive.
Through the shack's murky window
    we see her dark form move.
She opens the unsprung door,
    offers her creaky smile; we hunch

inside, hair dusting the low
    lintel, breathe in apples,
ask for Mullins—*Rusty Coats*,
    she mumbles, loads them into bushel
baskets; we hand her folded cash,
    lug the haul to the trunk, nod,
a shadow waving, pull away.

Down the road the Caney Fork.
    We glimpse fishermen, their waders and gear.
You cut the engine. I choose to wait
    on the bank, you follow the cascades,
navigate the jagged rocks half-way
    across, and beyond, noting the river's
level, the anglers' netted catch.
    I watch a heron stalk, dive,
swallow a small bream. The bird
    ruptures the air as it rises, marks
time in high breeze, finds
    the tree line's gap, disappears
over the bluff. I blink, scan
    for your silhouette, framed in a plot of sun
against cliffs where river widens, sky
    opens. You are a shade dancing
in light, a paper figure flitting
    on wire. I picture the wire thickening
to rope, me pulling your body,
    hand over hand, back to shore.

The retreating beats of the bird's
	wings echo. I think of the apple
woman, dilapidated shed, pungent
	harvest—the honeyed zest of my mother's
apple tart, her ashes strewn
	under a broad maple last January.
I want to hear you breathe,
	slide my fingers through your arms,
lock them between the shoulder blades.
	Distance and time, a heron's flight—
its absence, perhaps its return. I want
	to glide across that stretch of miles
back to the grizzled woman sorting
	fruit, to catch her rusty voice,
see her wave us off again,
	the sleeves of her blowsy jacket fanning
wind, a winter sharp with apples.

Pillow

by Claire Taylor

Yes, my love
  I know
a pillow can be forts and mountains
stepping-stones that slide
on hardwood floors and end
in tears. a throw pillow
can be a cement mixer
who's mad at the dump truck body pillow
for running out of
breakfast cereal this morning
(your symbolism lacks subtlety)
but no, I do not know this thing
you call a molvar
no matter how often you repeat the word with
the arrogant confidence of a man I hope
you don't grow up to be

I pet the pillow like a dog
honk its horn, tell molvar
we should take a trip
to the grocery store, buy some more cereal
salt in an open wound. my mistake

oh, sweet boy
don't you know
a pillow is for resting
long minutes flow into hours
days, weeks, months, and
the years go by so fast
until molvar is a memory only
I will hold
like the weight of your soft head
echo of your scream
though we were both there
those nights
when a pillow was
a vessel for my tears

Changing Hearts
by David Watts

Yesterday we sat in the afternoon sun,
conscious how time was dissolving into the chill
of evening, sipping our cappuccino
or ginger ale between words
that my friend drew forth
like the inexplicable raising of nectar
into honey, and I heard for the second time
the news of his heart transplant,
details like a post card from a foreign country
navigating the impermanent collection of sludge and ether
I call my body, to the cabbage-like brain
swelling to make room for this surging astonishment.

He'd been lying on the slab, he said, stoned on Valium,
the surgeons dotted around the perimeter
discussing which parts of the dying man next door

they'd plant in him, removing the tattered bag
of his heart, lying-in like a newborn
in another man's dream. The surgeon from Texas
leaned in and said, *We're about to give you what you need.*

My friend woke in the astonished manner of expectation
when, met with the *un*expected, rises
to a broader view, alive and aware
of the vigorous pump and surge of his new heart,
a dying gift from a man who no longer had use for it,
whipping about like a catfish in a river cove.

My friend stopped his story then, and tilted his head.
You know, he said, *they never tell you
the identity of the person who gives you the heart,
but I awoke knowing his name and his three children.*

He grasped his teacup in both hands
the delicate way one handles a gardenia blossom
just petaling open.

The afternoon dimmed and turned to embrace
the inevitably of night as we lingered, squeezing
the paling moments for their last sweetwater
drippings, drawing into our bodies
what warmth we could.

Yet something far more than flesh and grit
was riding the chest of my friend,

sitting across from me, alive
in this world, augmented somehow.

There was a silence then,
nothing would do but silence
in which his story settled in me like my own new heart,
clinching and whispering,
as we rose and stretched and walked away
into the murmuring, breathing night.

For an Osage Orange Tree
(and the names she'll answer to)

by Angela Sue Winsor

When bending the wood ... the cells have memory,
which they try to return to ... they spring back.
—WoodWeb

Say *Bodark*—for a pretty-leafed thing.
Hers are shiny, narrow, smoothed
curves. Pretty useful, too. Ask the man
who'd use her. Strong wood, farm wood.
Ripe fruit, sweet juice to fill the bellies
of pigs, to shade a home, and rest beside
while he still thinks of her as pretty.

Say *Hedge Wood*—she remembers
the home she once hedged, protected.
The best memory of any wood, even
as the splintering started. The man's
hands, the wood shards, branches bent
behind her. She springs back, remembers.

Say *Bow Wood*—when she reserves
the right not to bow or be gas lit, wood-
flamed, but to barb with thorns and milk
sap of her own. Flowers; inconspicuous.
Fruits; garish-green, very conspicuous.
They fall in echoes, to be trampled, eaten.
Still, she reserves the right to grow them.

Say *Yellow Wood*—for decay resistance.
He strips her bare to make yellow-wood
walls, yellow-wood floors, yellow-wood
fence posts. With so little left on the bone,
he calls her a weed of pastures and ranges,
says she should go and feel free to decay.

Say *Mock-Orange*—but speak gently to
her, too. Still tough-boned wood, alone
in quiet grove now. Know her by her crown
of irregular, reaching branches. Her trunk-
spine, arched torso, deeply-furrowed bark.
Her roots laterally spread open, unable to
forget. She still thinks she has to sturdy
herself, spring back, remember everything.

The Noon Executions

by Susan M. Gelles

The noon executions had begun, and still his friends teased him about María del Río. He pretended to laugh, but his head ached. They didn't know the prisoners; they heard the shots, and the cheers, and every Saturday night they drank to celebrate the everlasting strength of the regime. But they had neither seen the faces nor heard the voices of the condemned men. In this respect Antonio differed from his friends, for every day he met with those who were to die.

The general had chosen him because everyone said he had beautiful handwriting: the clearest and yet most ornate in all the three towns. For ten years, he'd written the baptismal and marriage certificates for the church of Santa Teresa; he'd even painted the borders of these documents with a brush made from the hair of an ox. Now he sat behind a desk at the jail, in a room that somehow remained cool despite the summer heat, as one by one the condemned shuffled in and sank on the unyielding chair before him. Those who could not walk were dragged by soldiers, but in all cases their escorts left them alone with Antonio. The guards preferred to stand outside the door and observe the buzz of the large anteroom.

When he first assumed the role of state calligrapher, Antonio mostly gaped at the slumped figures. They were brought to the jail each night, crammed into small trucks. Some soldiers claimed the prisoners were dangerous revolutionaries from the far-off western coast. Others stated, with equal authority, that the prisoners were criminals who had hidden in the mountains. Antonio could, perhaps, have determined the truth, but the list of approved questions for interrogation did not cover place of origin.

For the first three days of the noon executions, Antonio did not ask the prisoners anything at all. He sat behind his desk, fiddling with the sleek black pen that was much smarter than the worn brushes he'd used for church documents. He tried to look everywhere but at whichever man sat before him. The calligrapher watched the clock on the wall swing a copper pendulum back and forth. He tried to appreciate the yellow sunlight that bathed the room and which made it irrelevant that here, as in all the towns, the electricity could not be relied upon. Inevitably, however, he would find himself staring at the prisoners, who themselves mostly gazed at the floor's wide planks. I am not like them, thought Antonio. They sought trouble, but I live in the same house in which I grew up, and I bother no one. I do not ask: what lies across the sea; or, how may I find the treasures hidden in the tombs of kings. I do not ask: what if.

But because Antonio only stared at the prisoners and admired the clean shape of his pen, he failed to ask the requisite questions. Then at night he had to invent answers in his home, a four-room wooden shack that rested upon high stilts about a mile outside the town that held the jail. He willed his candle not to expire until he had conjured up the names of parents and spouses and children, varieties of occupation, and reasons for betraying the state. He knew no one would discover the falsity of what he wrote: the purpose of his records was not to provide clues for further arrests, which occurred according to a pattern known only to those in charge. Instead, as the general rather impressively explained, the red, leather-bound volume Antonio filled with his beautiful handwriting would one day go on permanent display inside a glass case at the museum. Future generations, said the general, would admire the state's perfect marriage of discipline and art.

To avoid losing sleep to invention, Antonio resolved to place the burden of revelation on those whom the state had chosen to bear it. Thus, on the fourth day of the noon executions, as the first enemy collapsed onto the empty chair, Antonio picked up his pen and said, firmly, "Name."

"José Santiago," was the faint reply.

"Age."

"Thirty-four."

"Occupation."

José Santiago lifted his head and smiled a little through broken teeth. "Cynic."

Antonio glanced at him, noted the man's bare feet, and wrote, "Shoemaker." Then he said, "Parents."

"None."

"Spouse."

José Santiago chortled. "None."

"Children."

The prisoner wiped his mouth. "None."

Antonio turned the page. "Reasons for betraying the state."

José Santiago said nothing.

"Reasons for betraying the state," said Antonio again, somewhat louder. José Santiago sighed and looked out the window, but it showed only the dusty courtyard where, in a few hours, he and two dozen other men would be shot. "There is no state," he said.

Antonio wrote, "Prisoner was recruited by an opposition party." The exchange seemed unsatisfactory. He was allotted twenty minutes per prisoner; scarcely ten minutes had passed, and José Santiago, staring at him, clearly expected something more.

The prisoner spoke and interrupted his thoughts. "What's your name?" asked José Santiago in a tone of some amusement.

Briefly Antonio worried that he might get in trouble if he answered, but he reassured himself that no harm could derive from altering the script with a man soon dead. "Antonio Sánchez."

"Age?"

"Thirty."

"Occupation?"

"Calligrapher."

"Parents?"

Antonio placed his pen on the desk at a neat right angle to the ledger.

"Parents?"

The calligrapher ran a finger along the gold-rimmed edge of the open page. "Dead," he said.

"Of course," said the prisoner. "Spouse? Is she dead, too?"

Antonio thought of María del Río, whom he had never even kissed. He remembered the curve of her hips; the solid thighs revealed when she raised her dress as she danced. His friends said she'd asked about him, that she wanted to know why he sat alone with his beer when everyone else danced and sang to celebrate victory. "We told her you don't know how to dance, that you can't sing," his friends had said, "and she claimed she'd teach you!"

"No spouse?" asked José Santiago.

"No."

"And childless."

"Correct."

José Santiago swayed; he half-turned and grasped the back of his chair. "Reasons for betraying the state?"

Antonio frowned.

"Reasons for—"

"Next!" called the calligrapher. The door swung open, and two young soldiers dragged José Santiago back to the holding pen to await the next round of executions.

Later, Antonio ate lunch at his desk and, as usual, kept his back to the window as feet scuffled across the courtyard. He waited, flinched at the loud crackle of guns, and then resumed his meal amid the sound of cheers. At precisely one o'clock, he called for the next prisoner.

A single guard hurried in, pushing a middle-aged man before him. The prisoner, not as battered as many of the others, seated himself as the guard closed the door.

"Name," said Antonio.

"My name is Luís Rivera, Antonio Sánchez."

Antonio looked up sharply. The prisoner wore a mustard-colored jacket, a dirty white shirt, and olive-green trousers; his face, with its hooded eyes and thick moustache, was unfamiliar.

"Do I know you?" asked Antonio.

"We know you," said Luís Rivera. "Before he died, José Santiago told the rest of us what he'd learned."

Silently, Antonio reproached himself for departing from official policy. But he knew of no actual prohibition against telling a prisoner his name or other such insignificant details. And the prisoners couldn't harm him.

"Age," said Antonio Sánchez.

"Forty-five."

"Occupation."

"I'm not as talented as you, I'm afraid." The prisoner leaned forward a little to better view the open volume on Antonio's desk. "I do find your calligraphy quite impressive."

"Occupation."

Luís Rivera seemed to consider. "Thief," he said, primly folding his hands.

Antonio hesitated, but then wrote "thief" in his beautiful, looping script. "Parents?"

"Dead," said the prisoner cheerfully.

"Spouse?"

"She's a rather private individual, and I neglected her shamefully. Perhaps just say I'm not married."

"Ana Rivera," wrote Antonio, borrowing the first name of one of his many cousins. "Children?" he asked.

"A disappointment. The eldest is secretary to the general. At least he had the good sense to use a false name."

"None," wrote Antonio. He'd arrived at the question he hated most. "Reasons for betraying the state?"

"Well," said Luís Rivera. "Where to begin."

Antonio waited, but the prisoner seemed to have forgotten him. "Reasons for—"

"Yes, yes," Luís Rivera said. "Well. Boredom, really. Treason promised a great deal of excitement. Plus," he sighed, "the general's wife is quite exquisite."

Antonio frowned at him; the prisoner gazed complacently back. The calligrapher picked up his pen and wrote, "Denies everything." The ledger was to reflect the execution only of confessed criminals, but surely no one would ever inspect page forty-seven out of a nine-hundred page book.

"And now I have some questions for you," said Luís Rivera. "Favorite color?"

Antonio put down his pen. "Orange."

"Favorite poet?"

"I don't read poetry."

"Ah, but you should. I particularly recommend the love poetry of the last century." The prisoner brushed some invisible lint from his sleeve. "And finally, share with me a memory of your boyhood. Tell me something you did when you were ten."

"I had no boyhood."

"Now, now. We just want a mere scrap of information. Climb any palm trees? Feed any chickens?"

"We?"

"It gets very dull down in the holding pen. Why, if you were to tell me about pulling a girl's pigtails, it would probably entertain us for a clear half hour."

Antonio pushed back his chair from his desk.

"How about age twelve?" persisted the prisoner.

"I left school at age twelve."

"Really! But you write so beautifully."

The calligrapher rose and shouted, "Next!" Instantly, the door opened, and a soldier pulled the prisoner from the room.

"A pleasure!" called Luís Rivera.

For the rest of the afternoon, each of the condemned men asked Antonio about himself. They never repeated a question, leading him to suspect they had agreed among themselves what each would ask. He searched for a purpose in their interrogation, but they never asked anything that could help them. By the end of the day, the prisoners had learned only trivia: that as a boy, he'd been fond of a white goat named Lucy; that his earliest memory was of peering through the gray netting that hung over his bed; that at night he prayed to the Blessed Virgin. He weighed one-hundred-forty pounds. His father had had blue eyes. By evening he felt unsettled, certain the prisoners were draining him of life through imperceptible drops. He stopped at the bar on his way home and drank his beer in a corner. The bar's electric lights, though flickering, always jolted him into a sullen wakefulness. "Dance, Antonio!" urged his friends. They stomped in a line, one man's hands upon the shoulders of the next, as María del Río sat on top of the piano and clapped.

The next day, the crows that pecked at unpromising dirt outside of the jail scattered as Antonio approached. Once inside, he found soldiers talking excitedly in the anteroom.

"Did you hear?" asked a stocky guard named Miguel Carrera.

"Hear what?" asked Antonio.

"Six prisoners tunneled out at midnight."

"How?"

"They may have had help on the inside." Miguel beamed, and Antonio thought he knew why: the execution of a few senior guards could easily result in a promotion for the young soldier. "They're somewhere in the forest," Miguel continued. "Maybe heading for the coast. We'll catch them, of course."

"Of course." Antonio cupped the cool metal doorknob of his office. "Why only six?"

Miguel shrugged. "Some would rather die here than be shot in the forest and eaten by dogs. And some hoped for clemency by staying."

"Will they get clemency?"

Miguel laughed heartily and slapped a fellow soldier on the back as an introduction to the story of the naïve calligrapher.

Antonio slipped into his office and sat down. He paused for a moment, as he did every morning, to sniff the air. He smelled wood dust, and something he wished were chalk, as in a schoolroom, but which instead suggested only an indefinite staleness. He fingered his slender pen and imagined that it held him aloft, sleeping upon a cloud.

He turned the ledger's pages: Luís Rivera, Hector López, Pablo Aguilar, Guillermo Martínez. These men, perhaps, were now crawling through brush, wading through streams, but really they weren't free at all, because they were running away, and there would always be something to run away from, and that something would never halt the chase. The regime's reach was wide; everyone knew stories of people knifed on the street, or found dead beneath bridges, even across oceans in far-away cities where they must have thought: here I am safe; here I may rest. Better, thought Antonio, to remain in one place; to scratch ink upon a page; to ask only what is permitted and then not care about the answers.

But he could not resist questioning a prisoner about the previous night's escape and whether, in particular, Luís Rivera had fled or remained.

"He was the first to climb down the hole," said the prisoner, a short, bald man who held his broken arm against his chest.

Antonio thought of Luís Rivera and his jaunty air and felt, somehow, fooled.

"He told us you would ask about him," continued the prisoner. "He left you a message."

The calligrapher waited, but the man said nothing. "Well?" asked Antonio.

"He said," the prisoner lowered his voice confidentially, "that a man who loves both the color orange and the Blessed Virgin need not be lost. And he said he hoped to see you again."

"He's dead," said Antonio, picking up his pen.

"No. Luís Rivera has powerful friends. He escaped. He won't die."

"Name," said Antonio.

The days blurred together. The first week of the noon executions passed, and the second began. Antonio, flipping through the ledger, could not match names to faces. In the evenings, as he walked past the wilting mango trees, he sometimes thought he heard in the croaking of frogs a note of rebuke. Once or twice he sensed a purposeful rustle amid the tall grasses, but he sped up at such times, and no one ever appeared. As he lay in bed, he tried to pray to the Mother of God, but he feared she couldn't hear him. His life seemed filled with the incessant murmur of other men's voices, and those voices paused only for the awful punctuation of guns.

Toward the end of the second week of the noon executions, as the calligrapher arrived for the day's interviews, the soldier Miguel called to him.

"Did you hear? The general's wife has run away."

"To where?" Already Antonio found it easy to forget the world held more than his home, the bar, and the jail.

"Straight into the arms of another man."

"Who would dare?"

"They'll catch him," said Miguel. "Then it will get interesting around here. That interview, I'll attend!"

On Saturday evening, Antonio sat in his customary seat in the bar's darkest corner. The crowd sang of victory and of love. Suddenly the pianist, a quick-witted man, stopped playing. The general and two of his officers entered the bar.

Everyone stood up. The general, reputed to be rather easygoing despite his high rank, made a gesture, and everyone sat down. At a nod from one of the officers, the pianist commenced a lively tune.

The crowd shuddered with a tentative relief. Drinks were poured; laughter bubbled through the room. A man pulled his girlfriend on to the dance floor, and other couples joined them. María del Río stood and chatted with the pianist, occasionally displaying a fine row of white teeth.

Antonio saw the general say something to an officer, who then brought María del Río to the general's table. She accepted a glass of beer.

The calligrapher strained to listen.

"You're a beautiful woman," said the general.

"Thank you. But not everyone thinks so."

"Impossible."

María arched a lovely eyebrow. "Sitting behind you is a man who would rather drink alone than dance with me."

The general turned; Antonio hastily gulped his beer.

"I'll have him arrested," said the general.

Antonio's stomach tightened. But then the sound of María's laugh reminded him of pennies landing in a jar, and somehow, inexplicably, he relaxed a little.

"No," she said. "He's only stupid. He isn't," her eyes traveled over the general's uniform, "distinguished."

"For some women," said the general, "distinction isn't enough."

"Mmm," said María. She gazed adoringly at his large ears, his jowls, his graying hair. "I'm not some women."

"Let's dance," said the general.

Antonio watched the general's large red hands caress María's body. They danced closely together, María whispering in his ear.

One of Antonio's friends, Pedro López, drifted over to him.

"You missed your chance," Pedro said.

"I had no chance."

"Just promise me that tonight of all nights, when we close with the song celebrating the regime, you join in. Maybe even look a little enthusiastic."

"I can't sing."

"Mouth the words."

But Antonio decided not to stay until the end. He left hurriedly, pressing himself against the wall, hoping not to be noticed. Outside a thousand stars filled the sky. As the bar's door closed, the crowd's noise converted to a dull murmur, and he again heard the voices of the condemned whispering their names, lying about the existence of wives and children, as though disclosure mattered, as though it could change a thing. He himself continued to answer the prisoners' frivolous questions quite honestly, for what did it matter if anyone knew that his father had cut sugar cane, or that his mother had salved his bee stings with mud to extract the venom? The details of one person's life and another person's life were interchangeable; he would be Antonio Sanchez even if his father had raised pigs instead of swinging a machete. He would be alone even if the general had not danced with Maria.

The third week of the noon executions began. Antonio felt weary; almost two hundred pages of the ledger were covered in his script. He wondered for how long the noon executions would last: surely the regime could not pluck every man from his bed and shoot him? But then something terrible happened.

Antonio was questioning a prisoner when he heard a commotion in the anteroom.

"Idiots!" a man shouted. "Idiots!"

The calligrapher opened his office door a crack and peeped out.

The general was shaking first one guard and then another by the shoulders. "You had him here, and you let him escape!

Is this a playground? Are you not soldiers of the regime?" He looked about as soldiers ducked into closets and hid behind one another. "Where are the records?" he demanded. "Who interviewed the man?"

Miguel Carrera stepped forward. "The calligrapher spoke with Luís Rivera."

"I don't want to hear the man's name!" shouted the general. "Where are the records?"

As in a dream, Antonio Sánchez fully opened his door. The general blustered into the office, sat behind the desk, and grabbed the ledger. He turned the pages with a kind of slap.

"Where," said the general, in quiet, even tones that frightened the calligrapher more than the shouting, "are the records of"—here the general trembled—"the creature who seduced my wife?"

In a hollow voice, Antonio Sánchez said, "Page forty-seven."

The general read the forty-seventh page of the calligrapher's clear and beautiful handwriting.

"Did you write this?" said the general, tracing the letters with his beefy fingers.

"Yes, sir."

"All of it?"

"Yes, sir."

The general continued to stroke the page. "'Denies everything,'" he read aloud. "Why did you not record the man's reasons for betraying the state?"

Antonio opened his mouth, but no sound came.

"All of our criminals confess. Are you a propagandist?" The general rose and surveyed the calligrapher. His eyes narrowed. "Ah," he said softly. "The man who won't sing of victory, who won't dance. Well," and his voice hardened, "we'll see you dance tomorrow. Arrest this man!"

Two guards rushed into the office and seized Antonio by the arms. Miguel Carrera poked his head in to watch.

"You there," said the general to Miguel. "Interrogate the prisoners."

Miguel froze. Antonio knew the guard was wondering whether to consider this a promotion. Perhaps it was, for now Miguel would get to sit all day.

"Keep records," the general said. "Be thorough."

The guards dragged Antonio across the anteroom, through a small door, and down a flight of winding stairs. They flung him on the dirt floor and climbed back up. The door closed firmly behind them.

Slowly Antonio raised himself. Here and there, in the deepest shadows, sat perhaps two dozen men, ragged and bruised. Some men's eyes were closed, so that he couldn't tell if they were sleeping or dead.

"Welcome, Antonio Sánchez," said a gaunt figure.

The calligrapher recognized the speaker; he had interviewed the man only an hour earlier. Already he'd forgotten everything about him.

"I'm sorry," began Antonio by way of asking the prisoner to repeat his name, but the man waved his hand.

"You are to die tomorrow," the prisoner said.

Antonio wondered if he were expected to agree, but he refused to accept that he was himself condemned. There was the matter of his handwriting, the most beautiful in all the three towns. Miguel would scribble like the footprints of a peacock. The museum needed Antonio's art. The red-leather volume was unfinished.

"Who will remember you?" asked the gaunt prisoner.

Antonio sank to his knees: suddenly the room felt close and hot. He wiped his brow.

"Your parents are dead," the prisoner intoned, as though this was a chant he had learned and was reciting now as a requiem. "You have no spouse, no children. Your brothers and sisters are long lost. In a few hours, your friends will deny ever having known you. Who remembers you even at this moment?"

The calligrapher thought of all those baptismal and marriage certificates for the church of Santa Teresa, but he'd penned them in the quiet of his room, and they were all unsigned. Even the nine-hundred-page ledger contained details only of other men's lives.

"You were kind to us," said the prisoner.

"Kind?" asked Antonio.

"You didn't beat us."

Antonio remembered the general's instruction to Miguel: "Be thorough." But it had never occurred to the calligrapher to beat anyone.

"You didn't force us," the prisoner continued, "to reveal the names of our families."

Some of the other men murmured an approval.

"But who will remember you?" asked the prisoner again.

Antonio looked around him. Some of the men he vaguely recognized; others, he'd never met. The gray walls against which they rested glistened with damp. He became aware of a sour stench. No one left here except to confess and to die.

He felt dizzy and reached for the floor to steady himself.

"We knew you'd join us," said the prisoner a little sadly. "Luis Rivera said so. He said you were too good to stay out of trouble for long."

"I wasn't good," said Antonio. "I was sloppy."

"Good; sloppy. Does it matter? You left us alone, and yet you listened. A rare gift."

Antonio lay on the hard dirt and gazed at the brown rafters of the ceiling far above.

"Here is a story," said the prisoner soothingly. "There once lived a boy named Antonio Sánchez. His mother's name was Carmen; his father's name was Ricardo. His father had eyes the color of the summer sky. His mother kept her long hair piled on her head in a brown scarf. Every year, on the night before the Feast of the Three Kings, the boy would put under his bed a handful of grass for the Wise Men's camels. In the morning, the grass would be gone, and the boy would find an orange candy and three pennies."

Antonio began to weep.

The gaunt prisoner's voice droned on, and when it faltered, another prisoner took up the tale, and then another. The calligrapher's life spun out before him, and a thousand inconsequential details became one whole. He heard the story of a lonely man who prayed but did not believe he could be heard. Yet the condemned assured him that some-one had listened and, for a little while, until noon the next day, would remember.

In the morning, two guards hustled him up to his old of-fice. Miguel sat behind the desk and nodded pleasantly.

"Name? I know the answer, but I have to ask. Rules, you know."

"Antonio Sánchez." The calligrapher eased himself into a chair and saw that Miguel's writing was indeed an illegible mess.

"Age?"

"Thirty."

"Occupation?"

"Calligrapher."

"Parents?"

"Dead."

"Spouse?"

"None; children also none."

Miguel glanced up at him, then scribbled for a moment longer.

"Reasons for betraying the state?"

The infamous question, but Antonio Sanchez had failed to invent an answer for it.

"Reasons for betraying the state?"

The calligrapher thought. "How about—inattention to detail?"

Miguel frowned and wrote something that seemed too long to reflect Antonio's words. The calligrapher felt em-boldened.

"Miguel," he said gently, "what is your favorite color?"

The soldier stared at him. "Green. Why do you ask?"

Antonio shrugged. "Maybe it will matter someday."

"I don't see how. Well, take care. I hear it's all over very fast. Next!"

At two minutes to noon, guards dragged Antonio and two dozen other men across the courtyard. The calligrapher's hands were tied behind his back. He declined the offer of a blindfold and glimpsed the office where, only yesterday, he'd been eating his lunch at just this time.

Facing him were twelve guards holding rifles. Who are they, he wondered. Do they know how soon they will be pressed against this wall?

He said a quick prayer to the Blessed Virgin, and it seemed to him that this time she listened, for she answered with a thunderous roar.

"The Noon Executions" originally appeared in *Belmont Story Review*.

Silent Night

by Mary Liza Hartong

You wonder if you'll see Christine tonight or if she's still in California. You know nothing about California except that it grows oranges and you only know this because when your sister was little you had to fish one of those white produce stickers out of her mouth after your brother dared her to eat the rind along with the fruit. You try to picture Christine in an orange grove. Only you don't know what an orange grove looks like so you have to make it up. Maybe it's like the airport parking lot after a long trip. Every corner looks the same as the last. You walk and you walk and you walk and when you still can't find your car, you give up. By this logic, Christine probably won't be at your family's Christmas party, but you dress up just in case.

Where are you going? Mama says.

You tell her, *Out.*

Don't be late to the party.

You won't be.

And pick up some ice.

Plenty of ice outside but none of it will do. It's got too much road in it, too much car, too much bird-squirrel-possum-whatever-guts. Auntie TaTa likes her drinks to clink, not slosh. She keeps stepping over one dead husband to the next. Mama says, *One day she's going to trip.*

What you like about Christine is the way she walks heavy and talks loud. She would make a terrible upstairs neighbor, but she's the life of every party. And girls like Christine can always sing.

They say, *No, really. I'm awful.* But then, *Maybe just one song.*

The night you met her she asked if anybody knew *Don't Cry for Me Argentina* on the piano. Suddenly the spotlight landed on you. All those years of sitting next to Mrs. Hernandez on the piano bench, waiting for the seat to snap in half. All those times her hairy arms skittered across the keys like little dogs. The neighborhood was full of dogs like Mrs. Hernandez's arms, but none of them could play a waltz like her. You wanted to have that kind of power over the music, but you hated practicing.

Do it again, she'd say, *again, again.*

Your nightmares featured sheet music. But, look. Because of her, you were the one Christine wanted. The one she *needed.*

Tonight, you say a prayer for Mrs. Hernandez, who died last Easter. Patron saint of patience, over-indulger of Doritos. Crescendo, heart attack.

The best ice comes from the gas station.

Everybody knows this, Papa says.

You tell him you will be right back with the bags, but then you have to run your own errands. You're 17. At 17 you're allowed to have your own errands.

You forgot a present for Mama? Where do you think you're gonna find something special now?

She likes Sprite and pork rinds, yeah?

He says that's not funny, but hands you a ten-dollar bill and returns to his shoveling anyway. Winter has always been your favorite season, the quietest one. People drive less. Dogs hide under the bed and refuse to be walked. You've heard it's because of the snow, that it takes up so much room, the sound just gives up, packs its suitcase, and goes somewhere else. That's like Mama and Auntie TaTa at Christmas. Big, bossy ladies eleven months out of the year, but when the rest of the family comes to stay they get softer, softer, softer. *So nice to see you*, Mama says. *Have another cookie*, Auntie TaTa insists. Aunties and Uncles crowd the snowy street with their rust bucket cars. Someone knocks over the neighbor's baby Jesus. All is calm. All is bright.

What's shaking, Liberace? Was the first thing Christine said to you after *Don't Cry for Me Argentina*. It happened in March. Winter was still holding onto spring like a child who refuses to leave her blanket at home, and as you walked across the parking lot with your sheet music, almost to the bus stop, her voice came out of nowhere. You turned around.

Hey, You said cautiously.

Shorts and a yellow sweatshirt, that's all she had on.

I heard a rumor about you.

Old news.

Coming out in this town is like being the first person to jump into a lake, the one who tells everyone else if it's too shallow. The sort of information you could only convey by drowning. You didn't, though. Damn it, you swam. But it's just like Auntie TaTa says: the water's cold when you swim alone.

Christine held your gaze.

People spread rumors about me, too, you know.

No, they don't.

Well, She said, *they should.*

Christine Brighton? Kissing you? You wouldn't have believed it five minutes prior, but five days later you found yourself watching *16 Candles* in her parent's bed while they visited her grandmother in Santa Fe. The yellow sweatshirt should have told you *Slow down. Proceed with caution.* But it was already on the floor.

The Brightons owned a grand piano that nobody could play, so the moment her parents hefted their suitcases into the car for their next trip, Christine would sneak you in for a song. Forget romance. You couldn't get a kiss until you'd given a Gershwin. Sometimes you played hints like *All I Ask of You* and she'd counter with a request for *People Will Say We're In Love*, an exchange that basically meant keep your feelings down or the neighbors will hear. This went on for months. May, when Grandpa Brighton fell down the stairs and you spent the week kissing in every room of the house. July, when God blessed America and the fireworks drowned out your laughter. August, when you didn't hear the garage door opening. The day she left you played *Send in the Clowns* on your family's trusty upright, a song she would have hated, would have said, *Too sad! Give me something cheerful.*

*

You take the long way to Texaco to see if the lights are on at Christine's house. If her parents are happier now. If they think the new school is *working*. It's no secret you're still in love with her. Your family understands that some girls want to be with other girls—*Ay, sweetie, we get it! It's all on TV*—but what they don't understand is everything you've done since she left. *Where did our good girl go?* Down the street, into the carpeted basements of miscreants, losers, and deadbeats. You picked up a foul mouth from your neighbor, Stanley. You returned it the first time you called Mama a bitch and got slapped so hard you forgot your middle name. Smoking didn't stick either. Just the same old empty feeling, like reaching for change in the pocket of a coat and hitting the seam.

Come on, baby, just one song, Papa says.

But you haven't played the piano since August.

The lights are on at Christine's house. They even put up Santa.

What took you so long? Mama says as you kick the slush off your boots.

The kitchen is full of busy Aunties and clumsy Uncles. Mama tells you to make yourself useful, but the best you can do is answer the door when the first guest arrives, startling everyone with a shrill *ding-dong* and a Tupperware full of bourbon balls. Her coat forms the first layer on Mama and Papa's bed. Later there will be dozens. A whole stratum of cheap wool and patchy rabbit that will remain un-excavated until well after midnight.

The room grows louder with every new arrival. Mama says, *You shouldn't have* as people hand her bottles of wine and tins of butter cookies. She ushers the gifts to the kitchen to be opened and shared, all except for Mr. Romano's salted toffee, which she tucks under the Christmas tree skirt. She will have it for breakfast tomorrow, a secret that everybody knows. As you sneak a bourbon ball from the snack table, someone taps you on the shoulder. Busted.

Merry Christmas, baby.

Auntie TaTa wears black for dead Uncle Alfie and shows plenty of cleavage for whoever will become your next uncle. She smells like gossip and eggnog, but you know she'd give you a kidney if you asked.

Your little girlfriend is here.

You remind her that Christine is not your girlfriend anymore. Not since her parents sent her away and she let them.

Isn't this the season of forgiveness? Auntie TaTa asks.

I think you mean the season of giving.

So, give her forgiveness.

You wonder if she killed all those husbands like everybody says.

What happened to Uncle Alfie?

She tells you not everyone deserves to be forgiven.

A tipsy neighbor steers you towards the piano.

Jingle Bells! Silent night!

You beg off to the bathroom, say you'll be right back. But, before you can make it there, lock the door, try smoking again to see if third time's the charm, you collide with a familiar face. Fresh from the land of oranges, Christine looks prettier than ever. Her voice echoes louder than you remembered. Her shoes play drums with the hardwood floors. And when she says your name, you find it impossible to stay as mad at her as you promised yourself you would.

Can we go someplace alone? She asks.

No sense in playing hard to get; she is already holding your hand.

In this house, someplace alone is hard to find. You try the guest bedroom first, where a sullen Uncle Joseph exchanges his wine-splattered silk shirt for one of Papa's sweat-stained hand me downs. The basement teams with sugar-spun cousins wielding Nerf guns. Up the stairs and in the pantry, Nana and Pop Pop spar.

Get out! They say. *This is none of your business.*

So, you pick a coat, any coat, from the pile on the bed and walk out the front door.

Nowhere to go but back to Texaco. North Star, open 24 hours. Christine's coat, a fuzzy, brown duster property of Papa's barber, trails the snow like a sleigh. Your short mink stops at the hip. Funny how she used to draw the curtains before you could even speak and now her hand is the only thing keeping you warm. Maybe things are different now.

What's it like in California? You ask. *Hot? Beachy?*

Even the snow can't swallow the huge sound of Christine's laugh. She says California is more than just a postcard. More than just oranges, Hollywood. It's a feeling.

How do I explain? She wonders.

I don't know. I've never been.

You pump lukewarm coffee into Styrofoam cups. Ernie says it's on the house.

Okay, how about this: in California everybody does exactly what they want.

Not like here?

No, not like here at all.

You always pictured Christine getting lost in the orange grove, searching desperately for a way out, but with her sun-soaked hair and hearty grin you're finding it harder and harder to see her as a captive. She says she's learned to surf. Tells you the names of her friends. Devin, Stef, Mackenzie, Dee. People so different from you they sound pretend. You should sip your coffee as fast as you can, knowing the cold air will render it undrinkable in a few moments, but you hold out. When the coffee is gone, you will have to turn around and walk home. Will she still be with you?

Devin says I'm a natural surfer.

Really?

Most people try for weeks, but me, I just knew how.

Last Christmas croons from the Texaco loudspeakers like a bad omen. *Once bitten and twice shy.* A frosted U-Haul full of people stops to use the bathroom, their legs wobbly from hours of travel, their children tottering forth in bright coats. You wonder where this family is going on Christmas Eve, if it's much farther, if there's room in the inn tonight.

Hey, says Christine.

As she leans close you catch the soft, tropical notes of her perfume. Not the cheap stuff she used to wear but something new, the type of gift you would give someone for Christmas.

Someone you love. And, what? The girl who never kissed you in public all of a sudden finds the gas station private?

Wait.

What?

Before she can have you, you need to know. If people in California do exactly what they want, what exactly does she do in California?

Christine?

I have a boyfriend.

Isn't California supposed to be safe? Teeming with glitter and megaphones? What about that famous mayor? As you rush to explain its merits, you realize you know more about California than you thought. You picture long, fake eye-lashes on folks with beards, how happy those people must be.

So, what, you're just starting over as someone else?

Wouldn't you?

I'm actually pretty good with who I am.

Christine flirts with her shoes. And men, apparently.

But, I guess you're not?

She tosses her coffee back towards the trashcan where it misses with a loud *thunk*, revealing just how little she drank. If you're waiting for her to clean it up, dream on.

I want my life to be easy, She says.

You aren't the one who's hard.

*

By the time you make it home the coats on the bed have dwindled to a humble hill. Just the neighbors whose houses hug yours, the Aunties and Uncles who won't go home until their children ask for Santa's whereabouts, and Mr.

85

Hernandez, who still can't stand going to sleep alone. Mama lifts the snow-speckled mink off of you, shakes her head.

Welcome back, sticky fingers. Mrs. Holmes has been looking everywhere for this.

You tell her you're sorry. She doesn't believe a word of it until she gets a good look at your face. Then it's: Do you want a sip of brandy? How about some of her special toffee? Only, don't tell your brother and sister because if they find it they'll eat the whole box and make themselves sick.

Love is tough, baby. Ask your Auntie.

Ask me what?

Auntie TaTa catches on as fast as Mama. She shepherds you gently towards the piano, where *Silent Night* has been waiting patiently all this time. Listen to the voice of Mrs. Hernandez in your head. Place your thumb on middle C. Then, wait until the *shhhhh* has made its way through the room, dampening the last few conversations and lit cigars. Until the loudest thing in the room is the Christmas tree.

That's when you start to play.

Playground Doctrine
by Myna Chang

In the grit of a 1975 farm town, 9-year-old girls weigh about 60 pounds, even wicked little girls with bad women for mommas, divorced mommas, but the boys that age are bigger, taller, and they're allowed to bring their footballs to the playground, because there are no rules for boys on the playground, they can do whatever they want, after all, THE PLAYGROUND IS WHERE YOU LEARN ABOUT YOUR-SELF, Mrs. Gibson says, the boys can kick and hit and play with their blue Nerf footballs because THAT'S WHERE YOU FIGURE OUT WHO YOU ARE;

but girls can't bring toys outside, especially Barbie dolls, everyone knows Barbie will get broken—it's her own fault— even when Barbie tries to stay away from the boys, especially when Barbie hides, she still gets hit and kicked, she still gets broken, and teacher says YOU KNOW BETTER THAN TO BRING A DOLL TO THE PLAYGROUND, WHAT DID

YOU THINK WAS GONNA HAPPEN, YOU WICKED LITTLE GIRL? and THE BOYS ARE JUST DOING WHAT BOYS DO, YOU'RE NOT REALLY HURT, QUIT WHINING;

so I try not to be wicked, I really do, but John finds me every day and punches my arms, kicks my legs, leaves his mark, every recess he laughs, and I tell him he sounds like Susie Wagner's dad's goat because I can't stand his bleating jeer in my ears anymore, so he hits me in the chest, aims for my scratchy training bra, where my breasts are trying to bloom, and maybe the impact knocks me down, I can't be sure, all I see is black, swirling tight, pierced with pinprick mercury bursts, dark sky, stars sharp and I curl in on myself, too late, again too late to dodge his fist, but I can still breathe so I do, I take a breath and uncoil, straighten my back and scream; but that's the wrong word for it: my noise is heavier, weightier, anguish and rage unleashed, dissonance exploding out of my 60 pound body like Coca-Cola from a shaken can, bubbles bursting, spewing IT HURTS, I HURT, YOU'RE BREAKING ME, and I forget that I'm a person, that I'm a wicked little girl with a bad woman for a momma, I'm nothing now but feral noise, a howl awakened, ripping black sky, striking wildly, connecting—

and then I feel it, that connection, it vibrates through me, the brilliant lightning crackle of John's nose, breaking cartilage, the clarion crunch of it, and my world goes pure—a respite, a beatitude—the mob of fourth graders frozen, Mrs. Gibson's mouth a soundless "o," nothing but bright silence for one shining heartbeat … two … and then that blessed crackle of lightning thunders through my bony knuckles already splattered with John's noseblood; and now he's the one screaming, yes, that's the correct word, he's the one on the ground, screaming, flailing, holding thick-fingered hands to his broken nose, and I think maybe I can leave this playground, maybe I'm already gone—

then Mrs. Gibson's slap connects with the side of my face, striking the heresy from me, slamming me back into my place, and her righteous adult fingers dig into the bruises bluing my arm as she drags me off the playground, gritted teeth, castigating with each step: GIRLS DON'T HIT BACK, a pronouncement, a commandment, and she stands me in the hall by the classroom door, puts me on display, a lesson, a warning, as the kids file past, girls wide-eyed, returning to their desks, and she makes a show of retrieving her paddle from its place of glory above the chalkboard, hung from the same hooks you'd hang your shotgun from, painted pink because pretty weapons wound deeper; and she holds the paddle high, parading it around the room before she comes back into the hall and makes me bend over so she can swat me hard enough to knock me to the floor, carpet burns on my hands; only then do I register the smack, an echo, but I can't start crying because I never stopped, and she pauses to stare at my jeans, wants to know why they're so dusty, why even my clothes are stained, but I can't answer because I've forgotten how to talk, don't remember I'm a person, so she leans over, grabs my shoulder, shakes me, a soda can, says ANSWER ME and I spew:

"I did!"

because I HAVE said it over and over, he's kicking me, playground grit on my legs, dirty shoes on my pants, you watch him do it but you don't care, that's just what boys do; and now she's eyeing the bruises on my arms with a look I've seen before, that twisted-lip lemon face that means my momma got a divorce so I must be wicked, too, and I know what she's thinking, that my momma made those bruises, and the mercury stars are back in my eyes because that's the worst thing, when they think your momma hits you, because it's not true, it was John, on the playground where you learn who you are, it was that boy who hits and kicks—not me, not my momma—it was him, IT WAS JOHN, AND YOU LET HIM DO IT! my bubbles burst AND YOU'RE THE BAD WOMAN! and Mrs. Gibson steps back, mouth in that "o" shape, but now the other teachers are in the hallway, watching, watching, so she says WASH YOUR FACE BEFORE YOU GO BACK TO CLASS, and I know she's right about the playground, so I wipe my hand across my face and smear it on Mrs. Gibson, my salt and snot staining her shimmery pink blouse, a statement, a revelation, and I crackle playground lightning as I step past her, and all of them, all 60 pounds of me.

"Playground Doctrine" originally appeared in ATLAS & ALICE.

Thank You, Girls!

by Dvora Wolff Rabino

My Dear Girls,
Marie Kondo says that before we consign even a ratty T-shirt from our dresser drawer or an unbecoming blouse from our closet to the giveaway or garbage bin, we should thank it for the service it provided. I can't say I've ever gone that far. Still, before the surgeon whisks the two of you off tomorrow to the Body Part Retirement Home in the Sky, I must pause to thank you for the ample curves with which you filled out those tops for most of my sixty-three years.

Please don't mistake my consent to this dismemberment for anger or apathy. It's not personal; it's just one more expression of an overall decluttering mission in this last act of my life. I'm culling needless items from kitchen, baths, and linen closets. I'm curating friendships. A few weeks ago I shredded half the papers in my file cabinets. I've been trying to shed a bit of tummy fat too. Now it's your turn to go.

I know it looks like the tumor's only in one of you, and a small bit of you at that, but given my personal and family stats, other parts of one or both of you could be next. Anyway, the two of you belong together. Separating you would be like sending two conjoined twins to opposite coasts.

Also, no offense, but you girls have become rather a weight around my neck. The cancer worries can get heavy, of course, but so can the flesh. It's as if I don't have two breasts anymore; I have a single pendulous bosom, like a peasant *bubby* from the old country. I'm tired of you guys hogging the entire screen of my little box on the computer during my pandemic Zoom and FaceTime chats. So I'll be taking the doctor up on his promise, after the demolition, to build me a set of younger, tighter, perkier breasts that may at least partially offset the aging look of my new, hairdresser-free gray hair and my sagging jowls.

Still: I place my hands together, palm to palm, and bow my head in thanks for the embers and fireworks of joy the two of you have sparked in me over the years.

Thank you, first, for budding and pushing outward in my skinny chest as my underarms and pubis sprouted their first tentative hairs and I began bleeding between my legs. At the time I probably complained that the growing pains kept me up at night. Now I realize what a privilege it was to welcome you into my body.

Thank you for causing the boys in junior high and high school to turn their heads. Without you and the hourglass figure you completed, I would have been not only mute but also invisible. But on days that I wore my body-hugging black leotard with the plunging scoop neck under the skirt or slacks that already emphasized my flat little tummy and rounded rear, the cute, popular boys would come up to my cafeteria table, lean over my shoulder, and casually chat me up. I understood that the suddenly feigned interest wasn't real or even about me, but somehow, even so, it made a shy, uptight teenage girl feel beautiful … and seen. It gave me hope.

Thank you for the titillating thrill you gave A, my college boyfriend, and later, in sequence, Husbands One and Two. Thank you for the dancing sparks and zaps of pleasure you helped them give me. Without you, my sex life would have been flat. You gave it that third dimension.

Thank you for allowing me to nourish two little ones through the first year of each of their lives. I fear I did not quite manage to give my children everything they needed and deserved as they grew, but with your help (and La Leche's), I did give the two of them that head start, that booster shot of nutrition, of immunity, and, more, of loving embrace. I still melt at the tactile memory of cradling my baby boy's and, two years later, his baby sister's dozy head in the crook of my arm while a heart-shaped mouth content-edly sucked away and a little, pudgy hand absently stroked my skin just above. Even now, as a grandmother, when I hear an infant cry, I feel you instinctively flush and swell in tender anticipation of that most intimate nurturing.

Thank you for the cleavage you provided. Thank you for the added bounce you gave my exercise sessions and even the sad but necessary lessons in gravity you imparted as you migrated south.

Thank you for growing and shrinking with the rest of me over the years. Somehow, until recently, you always kept pace with my body. And I realize that even your recent enormity is not your fault. The Entenmanns and Häagen-Dazs with which I pumped you up are totally on me.

Thank you for bearing with me as I forced you to be poked, probed, prodded, scanned, squeezed, and sometimes even stabbed. It couldn't have been easy. But you were stalwart and forbearing through and through.

Thank you, finally, for respecting my decision to say good-bye.

Now sprout your wings and take to the skies.

Love always,

Dvora

My Stepmother, Myself

by Abi Stephenson

She didn't have to love me. Biology didn't force her hand the way it does for mothers. She didn't gaze into the cradle at a miniature reflection, or see me crown between her thighs all bloody and self-made. I walked into her life looking like my mother; a fleshly reminder of her husband's lust for another, and old enough for lust myself.

I preferred her to the French flight attendant who came before, even though Lou was beautiful and bought me expensive perfume I was too young to wear. Jane didn't try to win me over, and it reassured me to sense that she wouldn't care if she didn't. She was much cooler than me in that way, with my need to be liked even by cold-callers and sales assistants. She was beautiful too, but in the way of women who get called handsome, not pretty. There was a suggestion of Princess Di about her hair and eyes, and her limbs were long and brown, even in winter. My mother supported my devotion to my father's wife in that she never criticised or condemned it, but in our lives, Jane was a topic only ever introduced by me.

I was never jealous of my stepmother. I was furiously jealous of the girlfriends, of the love my father showed them, but I never begrudged Jane her portion. I saw how easy it would have been to fall for her—she never courted affection or praise and was the more irresistible for it. She smelt like the Kenzo perfume in the poppy bottle, with spicy notes of Silk Cut and something horsey underneath. The cocktail of fags, flowers and equestrian life made her seem both glamorous and practical—a woman who could shovel shit from a stable and drink champagne at sundown. I can't stand your perfume, she said to me, when I was eighteen and trying to impress an unimpressible older man with YSL Paris. It makes me sneeze, she said, and roses are for old ladies anyway. When we went to Paris—Paris!—the unimpressible man told me to speak more quietly because I sounded brash and British and was drawing attention. When I crawled over to him in bed he sighed and said I was predictable; every time the lights went out I wanted sex and it was tedious. Jane told me later she thought he was a fussy old windbag. I loved her honesty, but not his.

The Silk Cuts caught up with her, and when the shadow first appeared on the scan, I took a month off work. I was 34 and she was a month off 60, which made it 18 years since we started loving each other. Jane had one biological child—a daughter—who was physically perfect but emotionally distant. Like a perfect sex-robot conjured up from a wet dream, she had dense fillers in her cheeks and lips, and perfect breasts under her Ralph Lauren riding tops. She lied about other things too, and Jane could not stand lies, even if she birthed the teller of them. My stepsister could not, or would not see the livers of other lives, and her solipsism left a wedge of daughterly space for me. Of course, I love her more than anything, Jane would say, but you're every bit as much my daughter too. She told me things she didn't share with her daughter, and when she was disappointed by her biological child, I determined to be compensation. Part of this came from a true and good place, but part of it came from an odious part that wanted to be loved best, most. Jane's love was worth competing for. On the day I married my husband I gave her a bracelet engraved with the words "More than DNA," and it glittered on her tanned wrist as she primped the flower girls and blew wreaths of smoke from the corner of her mouth.

At the beginning we had appetite for all of it. Over-photocopied hospital fact sheets called it The Battle, as if it were a military campaign and we could win or lose on our wits. That was the first of many smug cancer ubiquities that needled with their fake bravado. Months later Dad sidled up to me and said, sotto voce, if one more person says "ah, bless" to me I shall *scream.*

It was a teary, cinematic goodbye the night before The Surgery. But it's positively vampiric!—Dad said, holding another fact sheet in his veiny hands which suddenly seemed old, too old to be dealing with these sorts of facts. I made my special spaghetti with asparagus, peas, lemon zest, olive oil, parmesan and garlic—*it could be her last meal! I must rise to the occasion!*—and she worried about her garlic breath funking up the operating theatre. Would a man consider the comfort of the people gutting him like a fish? My elderly aunt coiled some greasy strands around her fork and recalled an article about surgeons who sew their patients up with scalpels and gauze inside them. Jane rolled her eyes at me and took a gulp from her super-sized wine glass.

But the lemon pasta was the first of many premature goodbyes. Because she survived that surgery—I told you you could do it!!—and I saw her wide smile again under the fluorescent strips of the ICU. My stepsister didn't come, but the ugly bit of me was glad she didn't. Space opened up again. The spare daughter could rush to the rescue, getting grim dopamine hits from being needed, from being there when others had failed. But there were more goodbyes, and each time into the breach I had to say it again—I love you! So much! You can do this! See you afterwards!—just in case. But later we barely said anything, embarrassed to haul out the old lines again. *I know,* we didn't say, blinking out our feelings in noiseless semaphore.

It started to get like when you say goodbye to an acquaintance in the supermarket, only to bump into them again by the tinned tuna. What's worse is she knew it: the false sunsets were driving us crazy. The photocopies didn't mention that—the social awkwardness of dying slowly. Like slapping your thighs, *I'm off!* only to have one more glass of wine and outstaying your host's will to entertain you. As she grew weaker, every time her eyes closed, I would think: *now?* only for her to blink herself awake and demand a glass of water or phone charger. I'm so frightened I'm going to find her dead, Dad said, but she never is. She burrowed into a nest of opiates and banal TV, spending hours watching *My 600lb life* and the *Real Housewives of New Jersey*. Not absorbing the best operas or teaching her stepdaughter how to live without her, but watching a half-tonne man cry as his thigh folds were sponged of something like cream cheese.

She once worked for a vet, and liked to scandalise us mid-dinner with tales of expunged anal glands and fungating abscesses. I'd ask her for ointments for my rashes or dry patches—even though I had my own—because I wanted her to go to the medicine cupboard and dig out the fluorescent orange tube with a picture of horse on the box. I'd fake horror, and she would tsk at my city ways. I wanted to show I was her daughter and that she had jurisdiction over my body too—that she was free to boss me just as my mother did. At university I Googled my sore throat symptoms and discovered I likely had stage 4 throat cancer. Sobbing, I begged her to come over, and she shone a torch down my throat and said—you're a bloody idiot, and what's more, you're a fool. We dined out on that story for years, but recently it's felt like a hypochondriac's reverse premonition—what wasn't in my throat was hiding in hers.

We sat in a circle by a fake skeleton and a loud COULD IT BE SEPSIS? poster. The bored hospital consultant used lay terms for Jane's body, and I knew it would enrage her. She's worked with a vet—she's basically a doctor! I said, smiling in what I hoped was a conspiratorial and charming way. Partly to get the doctor to use the correct terminology, partly because keeping it funny and light for everyone is what thoughtful women do.

I mean, of course she isn't actually, obviously, like you ... I know there's very rigorous training ... I trailed off, deflated by what I imagined she saw in me.

I see, said the consultant, in a way that seemed patronising to me, but almost certainly my husband wouldn't agree. What do you do? She said, leaning in towards Jane like an indulgent teacher.

I teach horses, said Jane, prone, dying and at a complete disadvantage.

The painkillers are muddling her, I said, because if Jane read as a fool they wouldn't treat her like the queen she was back in the real world, away from the smell of bleach and rubber sheets. I had given her syringes of liquid Oxycodone on the way, and she swallowed them like a grateful baby. She who bossed me most of my adult life, sat gurning in a wheelchair. She teaches horse-*riding*, Dad and I said in unison, not the horses themselves. We laughed loudly to oil the gears of a conversation no one wanted to have.

Jane and I shared so many secrets. Years earlier she called about some photographs she found. They were at the bottom of the guest room wardrobe where I'd stashed my belongings between house shares. We thought we were so powerful and womanly, the girls and I who posed for the creepy guy with the camera and the black drape backdrop. Jacinta's mum suggested him—she was an artist, and we wanted to be arty. I told him I worried my ribs stuck out too much when I arched my back in what I imagined was a sexual way. He said he liked that particularly. We were sixteen, and after the "shoot" in his basement he asked me to come back and model for him on my own, which I declined, quite breezily, thinking nothing but that I'd rather not. I'd forgotten all about the pictures until she called, when I was old enough to feel maternal toward the naked teens who thought they had the upper hand.

For God's sake hide these, she said, you'll give your poor Dad a heart attack if he sees them. She didn't ask any more questions—never did—and it was nice to have a secret together. I started smoking very late, and we hid that from Dad too, sneaking fag breaks together after mussels and white wine by the sea. Cemented by our vice, and aren't the slightly drunk talks over cigarettes always the best ones? What a blessing they seem now, the Jean-Luc Godard films that made me think smoking was so chic. I wouldn't swap those chats—that solidarity, that connection—even though it probably killed her, even though it may yet kill me.

We had other secrets too. In her mid-forties she fell pregnant, and they sat me down to tell me—baffled, apologetic. As if I were the parent and they the lustful teen tearaways. By the time they realised what her breasts were saying she was already quite far gone. There was no question of keeping it— his prostate drugs could cause birth defects, they said, and they were far too old anyway. He had to go abroad for work, but The Appointment couldn't be delayed. When he offered to stay, she refused, because anyone could see an offer was useless when what was needed was a declaration that brooked no argument. She told me the surgeon was cross and said he'd never do one that far gone again. That night I put on a CD by an indie band I liked, and realised too late that the first track was "All my Bastard Children are Gone." They weren't married then. From then on, she was loyal to me over anyone—more loyal than I deserved for one night of pizza and quiet company.

She's not old, I wanted to say to the handsome surgeon who directed everything to me. *She's not old, cancer has made her old, if you're thinking that it's her time it's not, it's not her time.* He didn't speak in the way you'd speak if you thought it was a tragedy, what was happening to her insides. Possibly because she had grey hair, possibly because the wheelchair, possibly because she had aged thirty years in six months. *J-Lo is only ten years younger than her, did you know that?* He probably only graduated last year and would talk about his day with the other junior doctors over beer pong. The expensive lipstick I smeared on her lips—*it will make you feel better, Vogue said so!*—looked like nothing so much as salmon-coloured denial as we talked about metastasizing things. I hated him but couldn't stop thinking about his arms, his hands, even as my husband was parking the car, even as Jane slipped away beside me. I flirted with him over her x-rays, over the talk of stents and time left on the earth. It was an automatic function that I couldn't seem to override.

"You're the very best part of our family," I wrote in their final anniversary card, because Dad was only able to write "Dear Jane. Happy Anniversary! Love, Me" in his. My husband came to the bedside too, and I wanted him to hold my hand but didn't want to ask, and anyway, asked and received is never as good as offered. We sat, the four of us, eating a cake the hospice chef baked especially, and which I greeted with a pantomime of oohs and ahhhs. It was a child's cake really, with hundreds and thousands, and Jane had to force it down what was left of her throat. I looked at my husband looking at her and wondered at which anniversary our marriage would end—who would die first, and in what way?

Death and so much waiting made an inventor of me, because when we had nearly run out of road I started coming up with plans; impossible, taboo plans. Like a desperate, incompetent entrepreneur, fucked-up ideas came to me at random moments. Could we do a life-swap gameshow for the suicidal and terminally ill? You don't want your life? No problem! Give it to someone who's desperately trying not to lose it! Or perhaps we could preserve bits of her body to stop the appalling waste of beauty. Her perfect breasts—so much fuller and more impressive than mine, and her slim, unwrinkled tummy—we could spare them from the fire and graft them onto me. Or we could do a trade with death and swap my ancient aunt, who was miserable and hated life and in any case, said she wished it was her who was dying. Perhaps a "baby on board" style bumper sticker but that you could wear, like a flag that would say "my wife/stepmother is dying in a hospice" so people weren't shitty to you in the supermarket.

We need screenwash, Dad said quietly, after we found out it had come back in her bones. Remind me to get screenwash. It was raining outside, and once we got into the hospice I could see she had given up. On the side table there was a "fun activities" form, and I grabbed it and said, Jane, pssst, be nice to me or I'll sign you up for a face mask making and socialising afternoon. But even though she laughed, she had shark eyes. She had called it a day—was packing up her ball and heading home. We told each other how much we loved each other, Dad watching on, crying silently. Later he told me he was getting too deaf and hadn't heard what we said, but he knew, he knew.

Each day a new bed would be empty where there once was a supine person and a crying family cluster. A sick stranger would arrive, and a fresh lot of grievers at the foot of the bed. What happened to the woman on the far right? I said. Dead, said Jane calmly, turning the page of a BRITNEY: INSIDE MY MELTDOWN article in OK magazine. One day she beckoned me closer to her bedside. She had stopped talking, mostly, so this was new. *This is it*, I thought, *this is where she tells me how to live without her*. I strained to hear, her voice raspy and competing with the beeps of white machines. Do you see those people, she whispered, you see those ones across the way? She took a deep breath. I nodded. On the other side, with the older lady? I nodded again. She took another shuddering breath. Yeah, well have you ever seen so many grown adults drink so much orange squash? She fell back against the pillow and rolled her eyes.

Perhaps it was in defiance of the fairytale convention— our love for each other. As girls, Jane and I had read so many stories about poisoned apples and wicked women spurning men's children. Where were the love stories like ours? The more the world expected us not to, the closer and more attached we became. She was more of a mother to me than my father was a father, and he knew it. Was I more of a daughter?

You're the only one she'll listen to, he'd say when she was depressed or drinking too much, but he was never jealous. He watched on, beaming, as his women grew around one another. Aged together. Two women forcing their way past biology, past childhood stories, past men.

I'll look after your babies, Jane had said, when she was well. I can't wait to be their grandmother. I thought of my almost-half-sibling, and wondered if she did the same. Around the time she became ill, my husband and I decided to "try," even though the word conjured up images of strained, desperate, fruitless sex. And it was so, because every month my period came, and I made no grandbabies for Jane. Someone in the marketing department had decided to put fun facts on each sanitary towel wrapper: "did you know you can save someone's life by putting a tampon in a gunshot wound?" the pink writing queried, as I stared at my knickers. But I couldn't save anybody's life, let alone start one from scratch.

I was holding a tin of tuna when he called me. Brine or oil? I had thought an important distinction, right before Dad said,

"She's gone."

And let the line go dead. That morning hundreds of perfectly round jellyfish had washed up on the beach, like someone had detonated a huge bomb underwater and the ocean had purged every creature within. I walked along the water's edge for miles, but the piles of jellyfish never petered out.

It was Dad's birthday the day we went to register Jane's death. "Oh! Happy Birthday!" said the registrar brightly when he gave his date of birth. All the rooms and hallways at the registry office were painted bubblegum pink, and in the building across the road a blow-up sex doll sat in the window, stunned, open-mouthed.

At the funeral a man no one recognised turned up with a single red rose. He had driven a long way and slept in his car the night before, according to someone. He wrote "What a girl, wow, what a girl! Love always, 'The Boxer'" in the remembrance book. Jane's sister thought he must have been a school boyfriend. The night before, I unpacked her hospice bag and found the lipstick I'd bought her. It still had all the hatched grooves in it from her cracked lips—her earthly echo preserved in the petal-pink wax. During the plague, they said peddlers sold trousers "left empty" by their inhabitants. Jane's clothes still hung in the wardrobe, her glasses sat, smudged, on the bedside table.

I am stuck on a single question as the wicker coffin floats by on a sea of shoulders, as I give the eulogy, as I wash down stale quiche and sandwiches, as I make small talk, as I put the kettle on, as I go upstairs, as I put on her left-empty tshirt and supermarket knickers to go to sleep. Do I use the balmy lipstick, and have the comfort of her lips on mine? Or do I save it, like a pencil rubbing, with her grooves there for ever? It smells like fresh, untainted apples.

Contributors

Allison Brice was raised in the deserts of Tucson, Arizona but resides in Washington, DC, where she teaches U.S. history. She has pieces published in *Orca*, *Typehouse Literary Magazine*, and *Metaphorosis Magazine*. She can be found on Twitter @_allisonbrice_

Writings by Lisa K. Buchanan have appeared in *Hippocampus*, *New Letters*, *Narrative*, *The Offing*, and *River Teeth/ Beautiful Things*. Awards include the Sweet 2020 Flash Nonfiction Contest (winner), The Bristol Short Story Prize (shortlist), and the Fish Short Memoir Prize (honorary mention). She likes The Charleston, black rice with butternut squash, Downward-Facing Dog, and breaking the Rule of Three. She lives in San Francisco. lisakbuchanan.com

Judith Waller Carroll is the author of *What You Saw and Still Remember*, a runner-up for the 2017 Main Street Rag Poetry

Award, *The Consolation of Roses*, winner of the 2015 Astounding Beauty Ruffian Press Poetry Prize, and *Walking in Early September* (Finishing Line Press, 2012). Her poems have been read by Garrison Keillor on The Writer's Almanac, published in numerous journals and anthologies, and nominated for the Pushcart Prize and Best of the Net.

Myna Chang writes flash and micro. Her work has been selected for *Best Small Fictions*, *Fractured Lit*, *X-R-A-Y Lit Mag*, and *The Citron Review*, among others. She lives in Maryland with her family. Read more at MynaChang.com or @MynaChang.

Danielle Claro writes short stories and nonfiction. Her work has been published in *McSweeney's*, *Real Simple*, *Domino*, and many other magazines. She is coauthor, with Dr. Frank Lipman, of *The New Health Rules*, a *New York Times* bestseller, and was founding editor-in-chief of the magazine *Breathe*.

Brendan Constantine's work has appeared in *Poetry*, *Tin House*, *Best American Poetry*, *Ploughshares*, and elsewhere. His most recent collection is *Bouncy Bounce* from Blue Horse Press. He has received support and commissions from The Getty Museum, The James Irvine Foundation, and the National Endowment for the Arts. A popular performer, Brendan has presented his work to audiences throughout the U.S. and Europe, also appearing on NPR's "All Things Considered," TED ED, numerous podcasts, and YouTube.

Brendan currently teaches at the Windward School and, since 2017, has been developing poetry workshops for people with Aphasia.

Tommy Dean is the author of two flash fiction chapbooks, *Special Like the People on TV* and *Covenants*. He lives in Indiana where he currently is the Editor at *Fractured Lit* and *Uncharted Magazine*. A recipient of the 2019 Lascaux Prize in Short Fiction, his writing can be found in *Best Microfiction 2019* and *2020, Best Small Fictions 2019, Monkeybicycle*, and *Atticus Review*. He has taught writing workshops for the Gotham Writers Workshop, the Barrelhouse Conversations and Connections conference, and The Lafayette Writer's Workshop. Find him at tommydeanwriter.com and @TommyDeanWriter.

An engineer by education, a nonprofit fundraiser by profession, and a writer at heart, Peter Dudley's career has taken him from aerospace to dot-coms to corporate responsibility to nonprofits. Along the way, he's published four novels and a number of other works, raised two kids, brewed some beer, and tore his ACL playing soccer—twice. As the father of a transgender woman, Peter is a vocal ally and advocate for equality in all its dimensions. Find him online at peterdudley.com.

Rebecca Foust's books include *The Unexploded Ordnance Bin* and *Paradise Drive*. Recognitions include the CP Cavafy and James Hearst poetry prizes, the Lascaux Prize in Flash

Fiction, and fellowships from Hedgebrook, MacDowell, and Sewanee. Foust was Marin County Poet Laureate in 2017-19. She works as Poetry Editor for *Women's Voices for Change*, serves as an assistant Editor for *Narrative Magazine*, and is co-producer of a new series about poetry for Marin TV, "Rising Voices."

Susan Gelles's work has appeared in *The New York Times*, *Twins Magazine*, and other publications. Her story "The Noon Executions" previously appeared in slightly altered form in *The Belmont Story Review*. She earned her MFA in creative writing at Columbia University.

Kari Gunter-Seymour is the Poet Laureate of Ohio and a recipient of a 2021 Academy of American Poets Laureate Fellowship and the 2021 Lascaux Prize in Poetry. Her collections include *A Place So Deep Inside America It Can't Be Seen*, winner of the 2020 Ohio Poet of the Year Award and *Serving*. Her poems have appeared in numerous journals and publications including *New Ohio Review*, *Rattle*, *ONE*, *The LA Times* and *The New York Times*. Her work has been featured on *Verse Daily*, *Cultural Daily*, *World Literature Today* and *Poem-a-Day*. A ninth generation Appalachian, she is the editor of *I Thought I Heard A Cardinal Sing: Ohio's Appalachian Voices* and the Women of Appalachia Project's anthology series, *Women Speak*.

Mary Liza Hartong is a writer and artist from Nashville, Tennessee. Her work has been published in *StyleBlueprint*,

Ember Chasm Review, and the *Portable Stories Series*. When she's not writing you can find her combing the local antique mall for treasures.

Molly Lanzarotta writes poetry and fiction. Recognitions in 2021 include the New Millennium Writing Award in Poetry (finalist), Sunspot Lit's "Culmination" competition (finalist), and the Fish Flash Fiction Prize (shortlist). Her work has appeared or is forthcoming in *The Rumpus, Terrain.org, The Vestal Review, Cimarron Review, Carolina Quarterly*, the anthologies *Snow Crow* and *Brevity and Echo*, and the book *What If?* Visit mollylanzarotta.com.

Christina Litchfield is a second-year PhD Creative Writing student at Binghamton University and an online writing instructor at Arizona State University. Her creative nonfiction has appeared in *Snapdragon: A Journal of Art & Healing*.

Laurie Marshall is a writer and artist working in Northwest Arkansas. She's a reader for *Fractured Lit* and *Longleaf Review*, and her words and art have been published in *Emerge Literary Journal, Stanchion, Bending Genres, Twin Pies Literary*, and *Flash Frog*, among others. Connect on Twitter @LaurieMMarshall.

Scudder Parker grew up on a family farm in North Danville VT. He's been a Protestant minister, state senator, utility regulator, candidate for Governor, consultant on energy efficiency and renewable energy, and is now a full-time poet and writer. Scudder Parker's work has appeared in *The Sun, Vermont Life, Northern Woodlands, Twyckenham, Eclectica Magazine*, and elsewhere. His first volume of poetry, *Safe as Lightning*, was released in 2020 by Rootstock Publications. Both *The Poem of the World* and *Gratitude* previously appeared in *Crosswinds Poetry Journal*.

A New Yorker and recovering media lawyer, Dvora Wolff Rabino has been published in *The Ignatian Literary Magazine, Linden Avenue Literary Journal, Penmen Review, Santa Fe Writers Project*, and *Steam Ticket*, among other journals, and is a recipient of the *Inscape* Editor's Choice Award. Her work can also be found at dvorawolffrabinoauthor.com.

Kathleen Rooney is a founding editor of Rose Metal Press, a nonprofit publisher of literary work in hybrid genres, as well as a founding member of Poems While You Wait. Her most recent books include the novels *Lillian Boxfish Takes a Walk* (St. Martin's Press, 2017) and *Cher Ami and Major Whittlesey* (Penguin, 2020). Her latest poetry collection, *Where Are the Snows*, was chosen by Kazim Ali as the winner of the XJ Kennedy Prize and will be published by Texas Review Press in Fall 2022. She lives in Chicago with her spouse, the writer Martin Seay.

Mark Schimmoeller is the author of *Slowspoke: A Unicyclist's Guide to America*, a memoir that was shortlisted for the William Saroyan International Prize for Nonfiction. His short work has appeared in *Orion Magazine, Mudfish*, and elsewhere. He won the 2020 Mudfish Poetry Prize, judged by Erica Jong, and his novel *Rock, Sky, Girl* was longlisted for the 2021 Blue Pencil Agency First Novel Prize.

Claire Scott's work has appeared in *Atlanta Review, Bellevue Literary Review, New Ohio Review, Enizagam,* and *The Healing Muse,* among others. Claire is the author of *Waiting to be Called* and *Until I Couldn't.* She is the co-author of *Unfolding in Light: A Sisters' Journey in Photography and Poetry.*

Annette Sisson lives in Nashville, TN. Her poems can be found in *Birmingham Poetry Review, Passager, Nashville Review, Typishly, One,* and others. Her book *Small Fish in High Branches* is forthcoming from Glass Lyre Press (May 2022). Among other recognitions, she was a Mark Strand Poetry Scholar for the 2021 Sewanee Writers' Conference and a 2020 BOAAT Writing Fellow. You can see her work and her sweet dog Jasper at http://annettesisson.com.

Abi Stephenson is a producer of cultural events, literary pop-ups, festivals and smart-thinking animations. For over a decade she was one of the curators of the high-profile events programme at the Royal Society of Arts in London. She also edited and produced the award-winning RSA Animates and RSA Shorts series. She was a senior bookseller and events manager for many years. Find her on Twitter @AbiLStephenson.

Claire Taylor is a writer in Baltimore, MD. Her work has appeared in a variety of print and online publications and has received nominations for the Pushcart Prize and Best American Short Stories. She is the author of *Little Thoughts,* a collection of stories and poetry for kids. Find Claire at clairemtaylor.com and @ClaireM_Taylor.

David Watts's literary credits include seven books of poetry, three collections of short stories, two mystery novels, seven western novels, a Christmas memoir, and several essays. He is a medical doctor, a classically trained musician, inventor and former television personality and commentator for All Things Considered. He has received awards for his work in media, in medicine, and as a poet and author.

Angela Sue Winsor is a writer and photographer from South Florida. She currently lives, writes, and teaches in North Carolina where she is earning her MFA from the University of North Carolina, Greensboro. She holds an MA in English from Auburn University. Her writing has been featured in *Southern Humanities Review, Saw Palm,* and *NELLE.*

Made in the USA
Middletown, DE
28 June 2022